The Broken Spears

With a Foreword by
J. JORGE KLOR DE ALVA

Translated from Nahuatl into Spanish by
ANGEL MARIA GARIBAY K.

English Translation by
LYSANDER KEMP

Illustrations, adapted from original codices paintings, by
ALBERTO BELTRAN

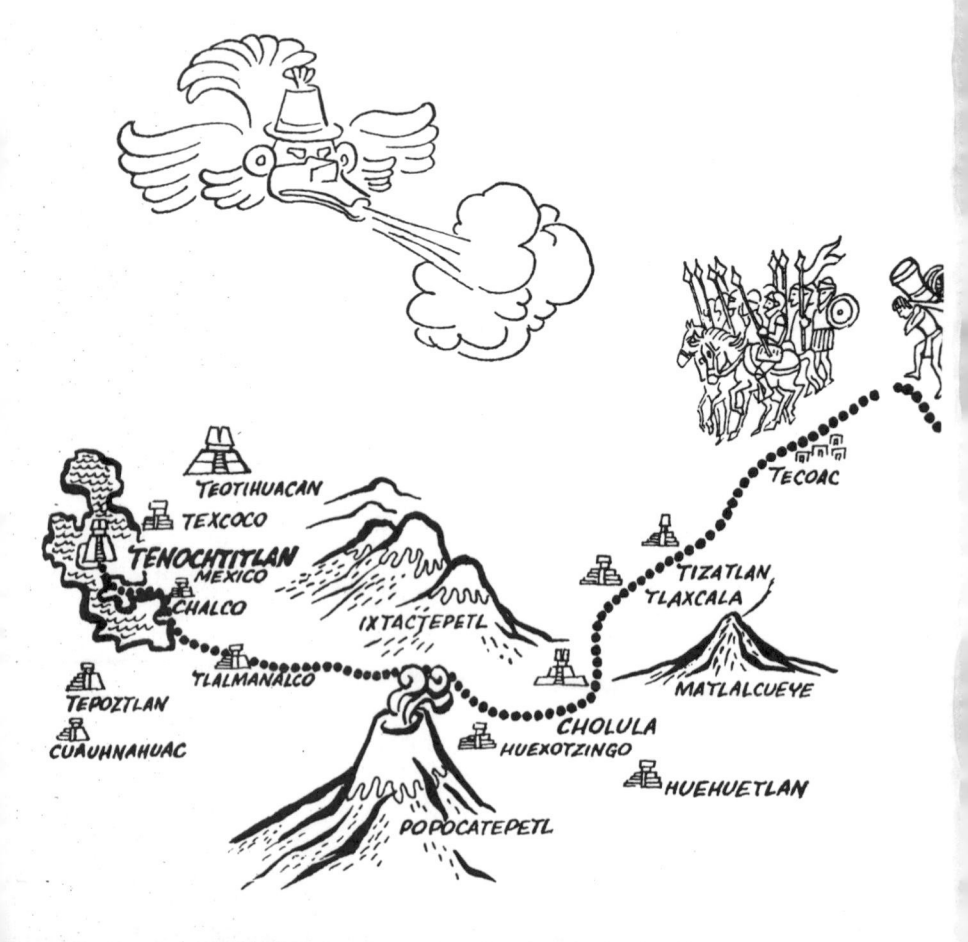

The Broken Spears

The Aztec Account of the Conquest of Mexico

EXPANDED AND UPDATED EDITION

Edited and with an Introduction by

MIGUEL LEON-PORTILLA

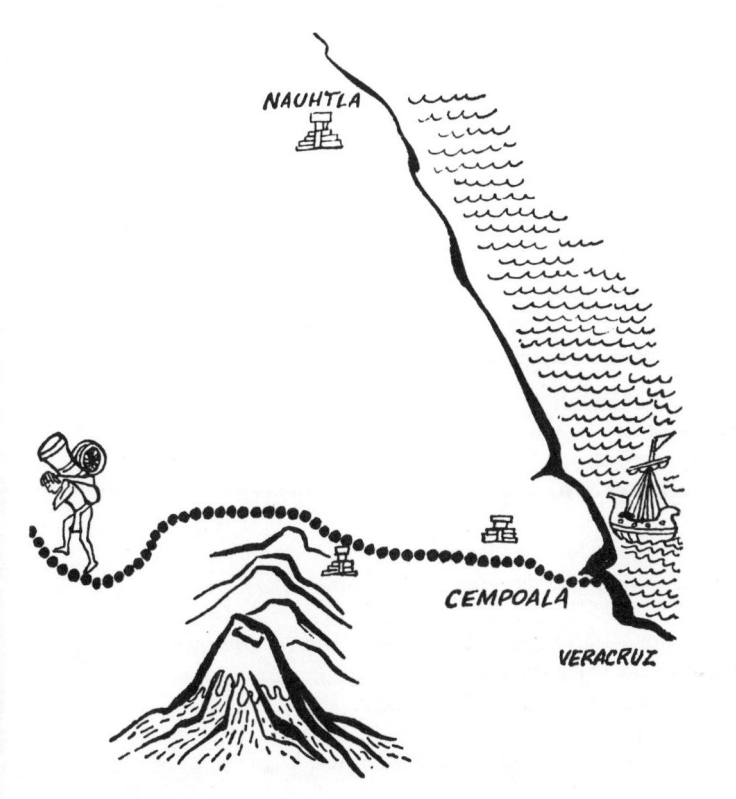

NAUHTLA

CEMPOALA

VERACRUZ

Beacon Press   Boston

Beacon Press
25 Beacon Street
Boston, Massachusetts 02108-2892

Beacon Press books
are published under the auspices of
the Unitarian Universalist Association of Congregations.

15 14   11 10 9 8

Library of Congress Cataloging-in-Publication Data

Visión de los vencidos. English
  The broken spears: the Aztec account of the conquest of Mexico /
edited with an introduction by Miguel León-Portilla; with a
foreword by J. Jorge Klor de Alva. — Expanded and updated ed.
    p. cm.
  Translation of: Visión de los vencidos.
  Includes bibliographical references (p.) and index.
  ISBN 978-0-8070-5500-7
  1. Mexico — History — Conquest, 1519–1540 — Sources.   2. Aztecs —
First contact with Occidental civilization — Sources.   3. Indians of
Mexico — First contact with Occidental civilization — Sources.
4. Aztec literature — Translations into Spanish.   5. Spanish
literature — Translations from Aztec.   I. León-Portilla, Miguel.
II. Title.
F1230.V5713   1992   91-35657
972'.02 — dc20   CIP

Contents

vi

Illustrations

Translator's Note

This translation is intended for the general reader rather than for the scholar. I have taken many small liberties with the originals, in the belief that a readable version of the drama presented in these documents would be more valuable than a literal rendering of their stylistic peculiarities. Here and there I have added a word or brief phrase to the text for the sake of clarity, and I have omitted words, sentences and even short paragraphs when they contributed nothing except confusion.

I am deeply grateful to Dr. Miguel Leon-Portilla for his generous assistance with a number of problems. If a translator may be permitted to dedicate his share of a book, this English version is dedicated to Soledad Duran, with gratitude and affection.

LYSANDER KEMP

Guadalajara, Jalisco
Mexico

Foreword

As is well known but quickly forgotten, the victors ordinarily write history. The losers are usually silenced or, if this is impossible, they are dismissed as liars, censored for being traitors, or left to circulate harmlessly in the confined spaces of the defeated. Bringing marginalized perspectives to light is therefore a revolutionary act of some importance: it can subvert dominant understandings, it might inspire other victims to raise their voice and pen their protests, and it always forces old histories to be rewritten to include or at least respond to the vision of the vanquished. For almost 450 years the history of the conquest of Mexico—perhaps the most consequential meeting of cultures ever—was based overwhelmingly on Spanish accounts. These had the effect of creating a series of false images, the most important being that the defeat of the Aztecs of Mexico-Tenochtitlan—always "by a handful of Spaniards"—meant the complete collapse of all native polities and civilization. Traditionalist authors wanted us to understand that Spaniards had triumphed against great odds and had succeeded in bringing about not only military and political conquests but also spiritual, linguistic, and cultural ones. A defeated, silent people, we were asked to believe, had been reduced to subservience and quickly disappeared as Indians to become mestizos, or had simply retreated into rural landscapes.

With probing intelligence, scholarly rigor, and humanist concern, Miguel Leon-Portilla, the dean of contemporary Nahua studies since 1956,[1] has been at the forefront of the struggle to bring the voices of past and present indigenous peoples of Mexico within hearing distance of the rest of the world. And no book has contributed more to this effort than this one. From the time *The Broken Spears* was first published in 1959—as *Visión de los vencidos* (Vision of the Vanquished)—hundreds of thousands of copies have appeared in Spanish alone, and many tens of thousands have been printed in French, Italian, German, Hebrew, Polish, Swedish, Hungarian, Serbo-

Croatian, Portuguese, Japanese, and Catalan. The present English edition, which first came out in 1962, has gone through numerous printings, with tens of thousands of copies sold since 1974. This great international reception among specialists and lay readers, the book's extraordinarily wide readership in Mexico, and its extensive use in universities and colleges throughout the United States are due to a number of related factors.

First, although the documents included in all editions prior to this one focus on the sixteenth century, they address topics that have become urgent throughout the so-called Third World in the last fifty years. Interest in the nature of native perspectives started when the decolonization of Asia, Africa, and the Middle East was set in motion at the end of World War II, and grew following the insurrections and revolutions of Latin America, beginning with Cuba's in 1959. Ever since, postcolonial nations and those wishing to overthrow oppressive governments have been searching for their indigenous truths and have been busily rewriting their (colonial) histories to match their postindependence aspirations. These efforts have included the quest for models to help make sense of the ways in which the dominated at home and abroad have resisted, adapted, and survived.

A remarkable discussion of how *The Broken Spears* has served as such a model is found in the prologue to its 1969 Cuban edition, written by one of El Salvador's greatest poets and popular historians, Roque Dalton.[2] The Central American author underlined the universality and inspirational nature of the book by observing that, although the documents referred to the conquest of Mexico, "their typicality is such that they constitute a valid testimony of the general conquest of the American continent. . . . [Indeed,] the set of confusions, acts of cowardice, heroisms, and resistances of the Mexicans is very representative of the corresponding attitudes of all the American peoples in the face of the arrival of the conqueror. . . . [And] these indigenous accounts and poems can contribute valuable data to use in locating the roots of the historical violence of Latin America." Dalton, who died in 1975 while fighting in his country's civil war, concludes by noting that, while Leon-Portilla had dedicated his book to students and nonspecialists, "the Cuban edition of these texts is dedicated to the Cuban and Latin American revolutionaries, especially those who, arms in hand, fight in the mountains and the cities against the conquerors [and] Tlaxcalans . . . of today, those who refuse to permit our historical epoch to close with a vision of defeat."

Second, for Mexicans on both sides of the border the story of the Aztecs (or Mexicas, as the residents of Mexico-Tenochtitlan called themselves) has played a critical historical and symbolic role in the formation of their collective identity. In particular, the tale of the Mexicas has served as the national "charter myth," standing behind every important nation-building legend or initiative. As a consequence, José Emilio Pacheco, one of Mexico's foremost writers, dared to speak for all Mexicans, Indians and mestizos, when claiming the book was "a great epic poem of the origins of our nationality." And he did not hesitate to add that it was "a classic book and an indispensable work for all Mexicans."[3] In support of this appraisal the National University of Mexico has published more copies of *The Broken Spears* than of any other text in its long history – hundreds of thousands, when in Mexico printings of nonfiction rarely number more than three thousand.

Third, the Nahuatl narratives in this collection, which now includes texts from the eighteenth and twentieth centuries, contribute to our understanding of some of the most important concerns in the world today, especially in the more multicultural nations of Europe and in the United States. These include the challenge of cultural pluralism and social diversity and the search for common ground in a sea of ethnic differences. Independent of nationality or political persuasion, readers who have an interest in the profound political, demographic, and cultural transformations of our anxious age have found something of importance in this work. Not surprisingly, it has become, as Pacheco claimed, a classic book, particularly among those in search of an affirming voice from a non-Western "other." In hundreds of U.S. college classes from coast to coast this book has created the occasion for fruitful conversation on the past and present nature of ethnic identity, nationalism, racial

xiii

conflict, and cultural resistance and adaptation. And as Dalton may have known, by making evident the ancient paths of tragedy, heroism, and resolve, this book has been an inspiration and a guide for U.S. Latinos, especially Chicanos (Mexican Americans), as they attempt to cope, endure, and triumph in the face of adversity or indifference.

Lastly, since its debut readers everywhere have recognized *The Broken Spears* as a "great read." Leon-Portilla, an eloquent writer and a masterful editor, has braided in chronological order a series of episodes – most of which were first translated by the pioneer of Nahuatl studies, Angel Ma. Garibay K. – that make the Nahua responses to the Spaniards, and each other, come alive with pain, pathos, desperation, and fear, along with powerful life-affirming doses of heroism, strength, and determination. The conquest of Mexico is freed from the triumphalist Spanish interpretations to which it has been moored for hundreds of years and set adrift in a sea of enigmas, contradictions, revisions, and discoveries when the Nahuas themselves are permitted to tell the tale their way and in their own words. But after all that has happened historically to the Aztecs and to their image in Western thought, what we mean when we say the Nahuas can now "tell the tale their way" is not obvious.

To Whom Can We Attribute the Vision of the Vanquished?

To understand the historical parameters of the documents in *The Broken Spears*, and thereby to elucidate what we mean by "the Aztec account of the conquest of Mexico," two related questions need to be examined. First, could the Nahuas have written in alphabetic writing ("in their own words") their view of the first encounter events, especially as early as 1528? Second, whose visions are actually presented in these documents?

Eyewitness accounts of the events and sentiments depicted in these documents are more likely to be reliable if the texts were written within twenty years of the fall of Tenochtitlan, that is, before

1541. Leon-Portilla claims that the descriptions taken from the anonymous manuscript of Tlatelolco (chapter 14) were in fact "written as early as 1528, only seven years after the fall of the city." If this is correct the work could surely contain accurate testimonies of people who personally took part in the defense of the Mexica capital. But is it historically possible for Nahuatl to have been written by Nahuas at such an early date? A few observations may help to answer this question.

Pedro de Gante, the well-known mendicant educator, wrote a letter in 1532 explaining to Emperor Charles V that since his arrival in New Spain nine years earlier he had learned Nahuatl and had had "the responsibility of teaching the children and young men to read and write" it. "And without lying," he added, "I can vouch that there are good writers and eloquent preachers . . . that if one did not see, one would not believe."[4] In another letter, written the same year and also addressed to the emperor, Fray Martín de Valencia and some fellow Franciscans state how since their arrival in 1524 they have taken young Nahua noblemen into their monasteries "and thereby with great labor we have taught them to read and write [Nahuatl] . . . and already they themselves have become teachers and preachers of their parents and elders."[5]

Furthermore, in his defense against the charges brought against him by the president of the First Audiencia (then the highest court and governing body in New Spain), Fray Juan de Zumárraga, the first bishop of Mexico, included the testimonies of people who spoke about the linguistic efforts of the earliest Franciscan missionaries. In this 1531 document a certain Juan de las Casas is said to have formally declared that following his arrival in Mexico City in 1526 "this witness has seen a written grammar used to teach the Indians to read and write. And that he has seen some of the said Indians write about the things of our Catholic faith in their language."[6]

Likewise, García Holguín, then a minor official in the city, stated that "this witness has seen that all the religious [mendicant friars] have learned the language of this New Spain [i.e., Nahuatl] and have produced a grammar in order to learn it better."

The list of witnesses continues, each faithfully attesting to the existence of early grammars and to the ability of Nahuas to write their language. Zumárraga's document thus confirms what later chroniclers, such as Fray Gerónimo de Mendieta would assert: From a very early date the Franciscans who arrived in 1524 learned the language, wrote grammars, and taught the natives to read and write it.[7] On the basis of these statements, and our recognition that the older elite students were already familiar with a literate world that included detailed historical records, we can feel confident that by 1528 there certainly could have been Nahuas capable of writing their language in Latin script.

Although documents in alphabetic Nahuatl do not become commonplace until the middle of the century, a related series of Nahuatl census records from the area of Cuernavaca appear to have been written between 1535 and 1545.[8] And in 1541 the cacique of Tlalmanalco, Francisco de Sandoval Acazitli (Acacitl), dictated a diary, which his secretary Gabriel Castañeda inscribed in Nahuatl, while on the expedition to Nueva Galicia led by Viceroy Antonio de Mendoza.[9] We also have various Nahuatl glosses in some codices (native picto-glyphic texts) that can reasonably be dated as prior to 1540. Consequently, although it is truly remarkable that the anonymous *Manuscrito de Tlatelolco*, quoted in chapter 14, could have been written almost ten years before the Cuernavaca censuses and Acazitli journal, it is perfectly reasonable to assume that we are not being misled when we read in the text that "this paper was written thus; it is already a long time that it was done here in Tlatelolco, in the year of 1528."[10]

I now turn to the second and more important question: Whose visions are actually presented in these documents?

Whether the manuscript of 1528 was penned at that early date, as seems possible, or a few years later, it is nonetheless the oldest surviving indigenous narrative account of the conquest of Mexico. However, the *icnocuicatl* (songs of sorrow), which make up the poems of chapters 14 and 15, may have originated at an even earlier date. Leon-Portilla notes, the "elegy for Tenochtitlan" ("broken spears") may have been conceived in 1524, while the poem titled "The Fall of Tenochtitlan" may date from the year before.[11] The exact years of composition, however, are not as important as the possibility that both poems reflect the sentiments of authors who could have taken part in the sad events and shared the sorrow expressed.

In this regard, it bears mentioning that the three poems in chapter 15 are found in the literary collection *Cantares Mexicanos*.[12] This means that the "songs" that are relevant to us in this compilation, those vivid verses from the oral tradition of the nobility of Tenochtitlan-Tlatelolco and perhaps Azcapotzalco, were collected and inscribed in alphabetic Nahuatl starting in the 1550s (the majority of them) and ending sometime in the early 1580s.[13] Poets who had been in their twenties at the time of the conquest, therefore, would only have been in their fifties when the bulk of the songs were written. These poets, to the extent permitted by the rapidly changing political and demographic conditions of the sixteenth century, would have been continuing the tradition of oral literature that had long enjoyed widespread support among the Nahuas, reflecting the social importance given to poetic composition and oral performance among preconquest Nahuas that the mestizo chronicler, Juan Bautista de Pomar, described in 1582:

To be esteemed and famous, a great effort was made by nobles and even commoners, if they were not dedicated to warfare, to compose songs in which they introduced as history many successful and adverse events, and notable deeds of the kings and illustrious and worthy people. And whoever reached perfection in this skill was recognized and greatly admired, because he would thereby almost immortalize with these songs the memory and fame of the things composed in them and thus would be rewarded, not only by the king, but by all the rest of the nobility.[14]

Thus the ancient and flourishing Nahua tradition of lyrical composition and oral performance noted by Pomar would have constituted a fertile environment in which, during and following the conquest, these bards could have produced stories and poems capturing the pathos, tragedy, and heroism of the defeated Mexicas and Tlatelolcas. This would be especially likely among the native nobility that was desirous of preserving the memory of a once glorious past and adamant about explaining (or excusing) the failure of Mexico-Tlatelolco to stand up to, or defeat, the Spanish-led forces of their indigenous enemies.

The songs of the *Cantares* appear to have been collected and inscribed by Nahua scholars working with the missionary-ethnographer Bernardino de Sahagún. These native researchers were also responsible for setting down on paper the content of Book 12 of the *Florentine Codex*, the major Nahuatl source of the accounts in this book. Along with rendering in script the texts of oral tradition, which included compositions from the preconquest, conquest, and subsequent periods, these indigenous investigators worked with picto-glyphic (and perhaps some alphabetic) documents. In turn, these were interpreted for them by over a dozen elders who, as Leon-Portilla affirms, were picked from among those best informed about the ancient practices and beliefs, and for being the most likely to have experienced the conquest in person. Sahagún himself wrote in the foreword to Book 12 that "this history . . . was written at a time when those who took part in the very Conquest were alive. . . . And those who gave this account [were] principal persons of good judgment, and it is believed they told all the truth."[15] In the foreword to the 1585 revision of the conquest story Sahagún reconfirms this point: "When this manuscript was written (which is now over thirty years ago [i.e., 1555]) everything was written in the Mexican language and was afterwards put into Spanish. Those who helped me write it were prominent elders, well versed in all matters . . . who were present in the war when this city [Tlatelolco] was conquered."[16]

It is of considerable significance that, like most of the germane poems in the *Cantares* collection, Book 12 is drawn primarily from the testimonies of informants from Tlatelolco and Tenochtitlan. And the same can be said for all other sustained Nahuatl narratives that appear to have been composed by eyewitnesses of the catastrophic events. For example, the second longest series of conquest episodes, the aptly titled "anonymous manuscript of 1528," is from Tlatelolco.

The so-called *Codex Aubin*, the *Anales de México y Tlatelolco*, and the pertinent sections of the *Códice Ramírez*, which although found in Spanish were most likely based on Nahuatl sources, are likewise of Tenochtitlan or Tlatelolco provenance (and the related episodes in Muñoz Camargo's *Historia de Tlaxcala* seem also to fall into this category since they appear to have been influenced by Book 12). The importance of this common origin is noted by the historian James Lockhart, who has argued that most indigenous histories from central Mexico, except those from Tenochtitlan/Tlatelolco, practically ignore the coming of the Spaniards, "show[ing] far more concern over Mexica inroads . . . in preconquest times than about the Spaniards." It follows, he concludes, that "only the Mexica and their closest associates put up prolonged resistance to the Spaniards, and only they made any at all detailed written record of the experience."[17] But what would have motivated them to do so?

Perhaps a better question is: Why, with the likely exception of the 1528 text, were all the relevant Mexica — i.e., Tenochca and Tlatelolca — narratives and legendary tales about the arrival of the Spaniards and the collapse of their two-part city written during or after the 1550s? One response is obvious. Although the most important accounts were written under the watchful eye of the missionaries, this was the time when Nahuatl alphabetic literacy extended beyond the Spanish centers of education and began to take on an independent life of its own in Indian towns. This was also a period of quick demographic decline due to widespread epidemics. The changing demography, in turn, was promoting local political rearrangements around newly organized indigenous municipal governments, which in turn were resulting in intensely assertive micropatriotisms. And all this was taking place as Nahua-Spanish contacts were becoming more frequent, longer lasting, and more complex.[18]

As is the case among all historians, the Nahua chroniclers selected episodes and details from the past with an eye to the present and future. The first two documents of chapter 16 reflect best how changing times could occasion the self-serving appropriation of alphabetic writing and precipitate the need to write the history of the past.[19] As Leon-Portilla states, within thirty-five years the Nahuas became adept not only at telling their own story through Latin script but at using such stories to protect their privileges and advocate for their interests. They not only petitioned the colonial officials in Mexico City but wrote letters to the emperor, asking for appointments to be made (in this case for Las Casas to be made protector of the Indians) and for grievances to be redressed. In the 1560 letter from the town council of Huejotzingo we read how Nahuas of one community could retell the conquest story in a way that would help erode the privileges obtained under the Spaniards by a competing municipality (Tlaxcala), while making their part in the wars appear worthy of favorable consideration (a reduction in tribute payments).

Although many of the descriptions in Book 12 and the 1528 manuscript are evidently those of specific eyewitnesses, or are reconstructions of their accounts, most are based on various anonymous stories that were retold and perhaps formally performed numerous times, with additions, modifications, inventions, and transpositions constantly enriching the recitations. As is typical in the Amerindian world, it was not a matter of individual, subjective perspectives being captured for posterity; instead, what we have in these conquest narratives are collective memories, reflecting common understandings, shared feelings, and group legends and mythologies. This, after all, is the way a dynamic oral tradition functions. But in the middle of the sixteenth-century the noblemen and literate members of the defeated communities were also stimulated to write by very pragmatic considerations: the need to safeguard their quickly slipping position as best they could, the need to excuse the strategic and military failure of Motecuhzoma and others, and, equally important, the need to express in redeeming terms the tragic fall of a glorious state.

It is of great importance to observe in the sixteenth-century texts that the Spaniards are rarely judged in moral terms, and Cortés is only sporadically considered a villain. It seems to have been commonly understood that the Spaniards did what any other group would have done or would have been expected to do if the opportunity had existed. Indeed, as the documents here reveal, when the occasion arose, the Tlaxcalans and Huexotzincas joined right in to defeat the Mexicas, their traditional foes. Each community strove to be an independent city-state. Each saw all others who were not their allies as the "other," whether Indian or Spanish. In this resides the central reason for the fall of Mexico-Tenochtitlan, and this reasoning helps to weave all the documents in this book into a single story: of defeat for some, of reaffirmation for others.

Beyond the Sixteenth Century

This timely new edition of *The Broken Spears* has been amply enriched by a concluding chapter that demonstrates how the revindicating voice of the Nahuas endured and continues to endure on the lips of the descendants of the vanquished. In these Nahuatl testimonies from the eighteenth and twentieth centuries we can witness not only the vitality of five hundred years of oral tradition focused on the conquest and its aftermath, but also the rhetorical force of over 460 years of literary composition in Nahuatl.

Today, in the poems of Joel Martínez Hernández, as in the eighteenth-century testimony from San Tomás Ajusco or the 1918 manifestos of Emiliano Zapata, a forceful, poetic discourse is placed at the service of the much-abused and frequently dismissed communities. Fighting against great odds, the one and a half million contemporary Nahuas are going beyond simply insisting on maintaining the integrity of their culture, by busily adding to their inheritance. Working with Professor Leon-Portilla in his seminar on Nahuatl culture and language at the National University of Mexico, a number of Nahua poets and historians have reappropriated ancient and colonial Nahua sources and have transformed them into living expressions of an indomitable spirit. Five hundred years after the encounter between the two worlds, ancient Nahua beliefs, modified by centuries of conflict, adaptation, and innovation, continue to inspire Nahuas to engage in what the editor of this book correctly describes as "the production of a new literature," or, as the Nahuas call it, a *Yancuic Tlahtolli*, a New Word.

Nahuas, however, are not the only ones who have benefited from Leon-Portilla's untiring examination of Nahua culture and colonial Mexico. Inspired primarily by his research and numerous publications, in the thirty years since *The Broken Spears* appeared Nahua studies have undergone a dramatic transformation. In Mexico, the United States, and Europe hundreds of scholars have set themselves to the task of researching into the Nahua past and present. Many, following Leon-Portilla's example, have learned the language and plunged into the sea of documents and chronicles that exist in Nahuatl. Thanks to this, today we are at last beginning to understand the intricacies of this amazing culture, which was the equal of any in Europe in moral refinement, artistic sensibility, social complexity, and political organization.

Because 1992 marks the quincentennial of Columbus's first voyage, it is particularly appropriate to introduce a new edition of this far-reaching book on "the encounter between the two worlds." As an intellectual, a humanist, and lifelong student of Amerindian cultures, Leon-Portilla, the first coordinator of Mexico's National Quincentenary Commission, has urged responsible debate and rational reflection on this emblematic and problematic moment. In many and varied forums, he has consistently rejected "celebrations" of "discoveries," championing instead thoughtful reassessments of the "encounter" that can lead us to more authentic, empathetic, and just understandings of the American past. These are admirable goals to which this book is a superb contribution.

J. JORGE KLOR DE ALVA

Princeton, New Jersey
September 1991

[1] See his doctoral dissertation, originally published in 1956, M. Leon-Portilla, *La filosofía náhuatl estudiada en sus fuentes*, 4th ed. (Mexico: Universidad Nacional Autónoma de México, 1974); first paperback edition in English *Aztec Thought and Culture: A Study of the Ancient Nahuatl Mind* (Norman: University of Oklahoma Press, 1990).

[2] M. Leon-Portilla, *Visión de los vencidos*, prologue by Roque Dalton (Havana: Casa de las Américas, 1969).

[3] Quoted in the prologue by R. Moreno de los Arcos, M. Leon-Portilla, *Visión de los vencidos*, rev. ed. (Mexico: Universidad Nacional Autónoma de México, 1989), p. 5. On the allure and significance of the "Aztecs" in Mexico and among Mexicans in the United States, see my introduction to M. Leon-Portilla, *The Aztec Image of Self and Society: An Introduction to Nahua Culture*, ed. J. J. Klor de Alva (Salt Lake City: University of Utah Press, 1992).

[4] *Cartas de Indias* (Madrid: Ediciones Atlas, 1974), p. 52.

[5] Toribio de Benavente (Motolinía), *Memoriales o libro de las cosas de la Nueva España y de los naturales de ella*, ed. E. O'Gorman (Mexico: Universidad Nacional Autónoma de México, 1971), pp. 439, 444.

[6] Legajo 1006, Archivo General de Indias, Seville. Quoted in A. H. de Leon-Portilla, *Tepuztlahcuilolli: Impresos en Náhuatl*, vol. 1, Historia y Bibliografía (Mexico: Universidad Nacional Autónoma de México, 1988), pp. 11 – 12.

[7] Gerónimo de Mendieta, *Historia eclesiástica indiana* (Mexico: Editorial Porrúa, 1971), pp. 550 – 53.

[8] See R. Haskett, *Indigenous Rulers: An Ethnohistory of Town Government in Colonial Cuernavaca* (Albuquerque: University of New Mexico Press, 1991); S. L. Cline, *The Book of Tributes: Early Sixteenth-Century Nahuatl Censuses from Morelos* (Los Angeles: UCLA Latin American Center, forthcoming).

[9] "Relación de la jornada que hizo D. Francisco de Sandoval Acazitli" in *Colección de documentos para la historia de México*, ed. J. García Icazbalceta, 2 vols. (Mexico: Editorial Porrúa, 1971), vol. 1, pp. xlv, 307 – 32.

[10] "Relato de la conquista por un autor anónimo de Tlatelolco," trans. Angel Ma. Garibay K., in Bernardino de Sahagún, *Historia general de las cosas de Nueva España*, 3rd. ed., ed. A. M. Garibay K. (Mexico: Editorial Porrúa, 1975), p. 822.

[11] His observation is based on A. M. Garibay K., *Historia de la literatura náhuatl*, vol. 2 (Mexico: Editorial Porrúa, 1971), p. 90. The translation to "broken spears" requires that "o" and "mitl" (arrow, dart, spear) be maintained separate in the Nahuatl text, which reads *auh in otlica o mitl xaxamantoc*. If the "o" and "mitl" are joined to read *omitl* (bone, awl), a second meaning, and perhaps an important intended pun, is found which would render the phrase: "broken bones lie in the road[s]."

[12] MS 1628 bis, Biblioteca Nacional, Mexico City. For a very controversial edition in English, see J. Bierhorst, *Cantares Mexicanos: Songs of the Aztecs* (Stanford: Stanford University Press, 1985).

[13] See J. Lockhart, "Care, Ingenuity, and Irresponsibility: The Bierhorst Edition of the *Cantares Mexicanos*," *Reviews in Anthropology* 16 (1991): 119 – 32; Gordon Brotherston, "Songs and Sagas of the Old New World," *Times Literary Supplement* (April 18, 1986), pp. 407 – 8.

[14] "Romances de los Señores de la Nueva España, Manuscrito de Juan Bautista Pomar, Tezcoco, 1582," in *Poesía náhuatl*, ed. and trans. A. M. Garibay K., 3 vols. (Mexico: Universidad Nacional Autónoma de México, 1964), vol. 1, p. 190.

[15] Bernardino de Sahagún, *Florentine Codex, Introductory Volume*, trans. and ed. A. J. O. Anderson and C. E. Dibble, no. 14, pt. 1 (Santa Fe and Salt Lake City: School of American Research and University of Utah Press, 1982), p. 101.

xxiii

[16] Bernardino de Sahagún, *Conquest of New Spain: 1585 Revision*, trans. Howard F. Cline, ed. S. L. Cline (Salt Lake City: University of Utah Press, 1989), pp. 2, 25.

[17] James Lockhart, "Sightings: Initial Nahua Responses to Spanish Culture," paper presented at the conference on Implicit Ethnographies: Encounters between Europeans and Other Peoples in the Wake of Columbus, Center for Early Modern History, University of Minnesota, Minneapolis, Minn., October 1990.

[18] See J. Lockhart, *The Nahuas after the Conquest: A Social and Cultural History of the Indians of Central Mexico, Sixteenth through Eighteenth Centuries* (Stanford: Stanford University Press, 1992).

[19] See J. J. Klor de Alva, "Language, Politics, and Translation: Colonial Discourse and Classical Nahuatl in New Spain," in *The Art of Translation: Voices from the Field*, ed. Rosanna Warren (Boston: Northeastern University Press, 1989), pp. 143 – 62.

Introduction

On November 8, 1519, the Spanish conquistadors first entered the great city of Mexico, the metropolis the Aztecs had built on a lake island. Don Hernando Cortes, who was accompanied by six hundred Spaniards and a great many native allies, at last could see for himself the temples and palaces about which he had heard so many marvels. The Spaniards arrived from the direction of Tlalpan, to the south of the city, passing across one of the wide causeways that connected the island with the mainland. When they reached a locality known as Xoloco, they were welcomed by the last of the Motecuhzomas,[1] who had come out to meet them in the belief that the white men must be Quetzalcoatl and other gods, returning at last from across the waters now known as the Gulf of Mexico. Thus Cortes and his men entered the city, not only as guests, but also as gods coming home. It was the first direct encounter between one of the most extraordinary pre-Columbian cultures and the strangers who would eventually destroy it.

Cortes landed on the coast at Veracruz on Good Friday, April 22, 1519; the Aztec capital surrendered to him on August 13, 1521. The events that took place between these two dates have been recounted in a number of chronicles and other writings, of which the best known are the letters Cortes wrote to King Charles V and the *True History of the Conquest of Mexico* by Bernal Diaz del Castillo. These two works, along with a few others also written by Spaniards, until now have been almost the only basis on which historians have judged the conquest of one of the greatest civilizations in pre-Columbian America.

But these chronicles present only one side of the story, that of the conquerors. For some reason—scorn, perhaps—historians have failed to consider that the conquered might have set down their own version in their own language. This book is the first to offer a selection from those indigenous accounts, some of them written as early as 1528, only seven years after the fall of the city. These writings make up a brief history of the Conquest as told by the victims, and include passages written by native priests and wise men who managed to survive the persecution and death that attended the final struggle. The manuscripts from which we have drawn are now preserved in a number of different libraries, of which the most important are the National Library in Paris, the Laurenziana Library in Florence and the library of the National Museum of Anthropology in Mexico City.

The Indian accounts of the Conquest contain many passages whose dramatic interest is equal to that of the great classical epics. As Homer, singing in the *Iliad* of the fall of Troy, depicted scenes of the most vivid tragic realism, so the native writers, masters of the black and red ink,[2] evoked the most dramatic moments of the Conquest. A few paragraphs from the documents presented in this book will make this clear.

The Indian chroniclers describe the beginning of the terrible slaughter perpetrated by Pedro de Alvarado in the patio of the main temple in Tenochtitlan. After mentioning the first rituals of the fiesta that was being celebrated—a fiesta in which "song was linked to song"—they tell how the Spaniards entered the sacred patio:

They ran in among the dancers, forcing their way to the place where the drums were played. They attacked the man who was drumming and cut off his arms. Then they cut off his head, and it rolled across the floor.

They attacked all the celebrants, stabbing them, spearing them, striking them with their swords. They attacked some of them from behind, and these fell instantly to the ground with their entrails hanging out. Others they beheaded: they cut off their heads, or split their heads to pieces.

They struck others in the shoulders, and their arms were torn from their bodies. They wounded some in the thigh and some in the calf. They slashed others in the abdomen, and their entrails all spilled to the ground. Some attempted to run away, but their intestines dragged as they ran; they seemed to tangle their feet in their own entrails. No matter how they tried to save themselves, they could find no escape.

Another passage, a masterpiece of the descriptive art of the Aztecs, shows how the Indians pictured the "stags or deer" on which the Spaniards rode. Motolinia, one of the early missionaries, wrote that the Indians "were filled with wonder to behold their horses, and the Spaniards riding on their backs." Now they present their own description, so vivid that it recalls another extraordinary picture of the horse, written in Hebrew by the author of the Book of Job. They report:

The "stags" came forward, carrying the soldiers on their backs. The soldiers were wearing cotton armor.[3] They bore their leather shields and their iron spears in their hands, but their swords hung down from the necks of the "stags."

These animals wear little bells, they are adorned with many little bells. When the "stags" gallop, the bells make a loud clamor, ringing and reverberating.

These "stags," these "horses," snort and bellow. They sweat a very great deal, the sweat pours from their bodies in streams. The foam from their muzzles drips onto the ground. It spills out in fat drops, like a lather of amole.[4]

They make a loud noise when they run; they make a great din, as if stones were raining on the earth. Then the ground is pitted and scarred where they set down their hooves. It opens wherever their hooves touch it.

The indigenous documents contain a number of scenes like these, so vivid that they seem to invite the artist to interpret them with his pen or brush. But to understand this epic narrative of the Conquest, it is important to know something of Aztec history, geography and culture. The following sketch is necessarily limited to the broad outlines, but at least it will provide a context in which the indigenous narratives can be seen more clearly.

Cultural Stages of Ancient Mexico

The grandeur that the conquistadors beheld in the Aztec capital was obviously not the result of spontaneous generation. It was the last phase of a long cultural sequence beginning well before the Christian era. In this brief review of the evolution of culture in ancient Mexico, we will attempt to correlate the various stages with well-known events in the history of the Old World.

Although man has existed on earth for at least half a million years, the first human beings to reach the American continent appear to have arrived only about twenty thousand years ago. Man is an even more recent phenomenon in the Valley of Mexico, since the most ancient human fossil—discovered in Tepexpan, near the famous pyramids of Teotihuacan—is probably no more than ten thousand years old.

The development of superior cultural forms also came much later in America than in the Old World. Egypt and Mesopotamia had contrived modes of writing as far back as the fourth millennium before Christ, but in America—specifically in Mexico—we must wait until the middle of the second millennium B.C. before we can discover the earliest vestiges of systematic agriculture and the making of pottery.

The most ancient architectural remains in Mexico, indicating the presence of ceremonial centers, date from about five hundred years before Christ, a time when the Old World had already heard the words of the Biblical prophets, and when the first pre-Socratic philosophers had already spoken in Greece. Perhaps the earliest cultural ferment of any importance in pre-Columbian Mexico took place on the coast of the Gulf of Mexico. A number of extraordinary artifacts have been found there, along with the oldest calendar inscription yet discovered. For lack of a better name, these mysterious artificers have been called the Olmecs, an Aztec word meaning "people of the region of rubber." At a later period their art, techniques and religious ideas influenced a number of groups which had migrated from the distant northern shores of the Pacific Ocean. This cultural influence was to have significant and widespread consequences.

At the beginning of the Christian era, while Rome was consolidating her empire and Christianity had begun to spread through the Mediterranean world, Mexico witnessed the emergence of what can also be called true empires. The foundations of the earliest sacred cities of the Mayas—Tikal, Uaxactun, Copan and Palenque —were constructed in the jungles of Central America. And in the central region of Mexico, about thirty-five miles north of the modern capital, the great "city of the gods"—Teotihuacan—began to rise. Its pyramids, palaces, sculptures, frescoes and inscriptions would become a paradigm and inspiration for the artists and artisans of later peoples. Many of its inscriptions and representations of the gods were reproduced in the Aztec art and codices of the Conquest period. The apogee of Mayan and Teotihuacan culture coincides in time with the fall of the Roman Empire.

During the fourth and fifth centuries A.D. inscriptions based on a partly ideographic, partly phonetic mode of writing became extremely abundant, especially among the Mayas. They testify to the fact that these cultures possessed a profound sense of time and history. The Mayan calendar is further proof, for it was slightly closer to the astronomical year than our own present-day calendar, and much closer than that being used in Europe at the same period.

The great ritual centers at Teotihuacan and in the Mayan area began to decline in the eighth and ninth centuries and were eventually abandoned. The causes are for the most part unknown. Some authors have attributed their downfall to the arrival of new tribes from the north; at least it is certain that the northern barbarians— like the Germanic tribes in the Roman world—were a constant threat to established cultures. In Europe the ninth century saw the consolidation of feudalism; a little later new kingdoms were founded within a cultural milieu composed of Greco-Roman and barbarian elements. A new state also arose in central Mexico and culturally it was also a composite, having been greatly influenced by the Teotihuacan civilization. This was the so-called "Toltec Empire," composed of people from the north who spoke the same Nahuatl tongue which a few centuries later became the language of the Aztecs.

The Toltecs settled in Tula, about fifty-five miles northeast of the City of Mexico, and under the aegis of their great culture-hero, Quetzalcoatl, they gradually extended the civilization created at Teotihuacan. A number of indigenous texts describe the Toltecs in detail: they were superb artisans, devout worshipers, skillful tradesmen—extraordinary persons in every way. Their prestige became so great that for the Aztecs the word "Toltec" was a synonym for "artist." The cultural achievements of the Toltecs spread far beyond their city at Tula; in fact their influence even reached down into Yucatan and Central America, where it can be clearly discerned in the Mayan religious center at Chichen-Itza. As a result of these Toltec influences, the Mayas experienced a major cultural renascence.

But Tula, like other cities before it, was finally abandoned, perhaps because of fresh invasions from the north. Quetzalcoatl departed eastward, promising that some day he would return from across the sea. The new arrivals adopted the cultures of Teotihuacan and the Toltecs, and a number of city-states began to form along the shores of the great lake in the Valley of Mexico. This was the beginning of another cultural renascence, almost exactly contemporaneous with the early Renaissance in Italy.

In the thirteenth century two of the city-states achieved considerable splendor. One of them, the famous Culhuacan, was located on the southern shore of the lake, near what is now the University of Mexico. Much of its greatness resulted from the fact that many of its inhabitants were of Toltec origin. The other state, Azcapotzalco, which now forms part of the northeastern sector of the capital, was a mixture of a great many ethnic groups. Its people were especially gifted as warriors and administrators, and Azcapotzalco therefore became a good deal more powerful than its neighbor to the south.

The Valley of Mexico

The Aztecs or Mexicas were the last of the many nomadic tribes to enter the Valley of Mexico from the north. They arrived during the middle of the thirteenth century, and attempted to settle in one or another of the flourishing city-states, but wherever they appeared, they were violently driven away as undesirable foreigners. It is true that they spoke the same language as the old Toltecs, but otherwise they were almost totally uncultured. The only heritage they brought with them, besides the Nahuatl tongue, was an indomitable will.

After a whole series of defeats and humiliations, the Aztecs succeeded in establishing themselves on an island in the lake; the ancient codices state that their city was founded in the year 1325. A little more than a century later, incredible as it may seem, this destitute tribe had been able to assimilate the old cultural traditions and, at the same time, to achieve complete independence. Then they began their career as conquerors, extending their rule from the Gulf coast to the Pacific and as far south as Guatemala— and again they accomplished all this in only one century. Their capital grew rich and powerful, much more powerful than Teotihuacan or Tula had ever been. Its temples, palaces and gardens were so magnificent that the Spanish conquistadors gaped in astonishment.

During this same period, however, the Old World had begun to discover new regions. Portuguese navigators reached Madeira and the Azores between 1416 and 1432—the first step toward the discovery of the New World. Other explorers crossed the Equator off the coast of Africa in about 1470, and in 1487 Bartolomew Diaz sailed as far as the Cape of Good Hope. Less than a decade later Christopher Columbus landed on the shores of America. Hence, the "explosion" which spread Aztec rule and planted Aztec culture over vast regions was contemporaneous with another expansionist movement, and the latter, with superior weapons, techniques and tactics, proved much the more powerful. When the Old World and the Aztecs in the New World met face to face on that November day in 1519, their attitudes toward each other were very different. The Aztecs, as we have said, thought the strangers were Quetzalcoatl and other gods returning from over the sea, while the Spaniards—despite their amazement at the splendors of Tenochtitlan—considered the Aztecs barbarians and thought only of seizing their riches and of forcing them to become Christians and Spanish subjects.

This confrontation, vividly described both by the conquistadors and the natives, was something more than a meeting between two expanding nations; it was the meeting of two radically dissimilar cultures, two radically different modes of interpreting existence. Spain had recently brought the long wars of reconquest against the Moors to a triumphant conclusion and was now the greatest power in Europe. The Aztec state had also reached a climax, and its magnificence was evident in its capital city and its vigorous religious, social, economic and political structure. To understand more clearly the tragic loss that resulted from the destruction of indigenous culture, it will be useful to view the great city as the "gods" viewed it before they leveled it to the ground.

Tenochtitlan, the Aztec Metropolis

The beginnings of the Aztec capital were very humble. It was founded on a low-lying island so undesirable that other tribes had not bothered to occupy it. The indigenous chronicles describe the difficulties with which the Aztecs managed to build a few miserable huts and a small altar to their supreme deity, the war-god Huitzilopochtli. But their fierce will overcame every obstacle. Less than two centuries later, the Spanish conquistador Bernal Diaz del Castillo thought that the wonders he beheld must be a dream. The Spaniards had been welcomed into the city as guests of Motecuhzoma, and a party of them—led by Cortes—climbed up to the flat top of the pyramid on which the main temple was built. They were met by the Aztec king himself, who pointed out the various sights.

Pre-Columbian Mexico-Tenochtitlan

So we stood looking about us, for that huge and cursed temple stood so high that from it one could see over everything very well, and we saw the three causeways which led into Mexico, that is the causeway of Iztapalapa by which we had entered four days before, and that of Tacuba, and that of Tepeaquilla, and we saw the fresh water that comes from Chapultepec which supplies the city, and we saw the bridges on the three causeways which were built at certain distances apart through which the water of the lake flowed in and out from one side to the other, and we beheld on that great lake a great multitude of canoes, some coming with supplies of food and others returning loaded with cargoes of merchandise; and we saw that from every house of that great city and of all the other cities that were built in the water it was impossible to pass from house to house, except by drawbridges which were made of wood or in canoes; and we saw in those cities Cues [temples] and oratories like towers and fortresses and all gleaming white, and it was a wonderful thing to behold; then the houses with flat roofs, and on the causeways other small towers and oratories which were like fortresses.

After having examined and considered all that we had seen we turned to look at the great market place and the crowds of people that were in it, some buying and others selling, so that the murmur and hum of their voices and words that they used could be heard more than a league off. Some of the soldiers among us who had been in many parts of the world, in Constantinople, and all over Italy, and in Rome, said that so large a market place and so full of people, and so well regulated and arranged, they had never beheld before.[5]

The Spanish soldier had good reasons for describing the city in such enthusiastic terms. Almost nothing remains today of what he saw, but his account is corroborated by other writings, ancient maps and archaeological investigations.

At the time of the Conquest, the area of the island on which the city stood had been increased by means of fills, until it comprised a more or less regular square measuring about two miles on each side. It was joined on the north to the island of Tlatelolco, originally an independent city, but annexed by the Aztecs in 1473. Tlatelolco was connected with the mainland by a causeway that ran to the sanctuary of the mother-goddess Tonantzin on the northern shore of the lake. At the present day the site of her temple is occupied by the Basilica of Tepeyac, dedicated to Mexico's patron saint, the Virgin of Guadalupe.

To the south of Tenochtitlan, another causeway—the one by which the Spaniards entered—joined the mainland at Iztapalapa. The eastern edge of the city bordered the wide expanse of the lake, and only during the clearest weather was it possible to see the city of Tezcoco, home of the famous poet-king Nezahualcoyotl, on the opposite shore. Finally, on the west, another causeway joined the city with the allied kingdom of Tlacopan or Tacuba; it was along this causeway that the Spaniards fled on the disastrous Night of Sorrows.

Tenochtitlan was divided into four great sections. To the northwest stood Cuepopan, "the place where flowers bloom," which now forms the *barrio* or sector known as Santa Maria la Redonda; to the southwest, Moyotlan, "the place of the gnats," later dedicated by the Spanish missionaries to the honor of St. John the Baptist; to the southeast, Teopan, "the place of the gods," which included the precinct of the main temple and which was known in colonial times by the name of San Pablo; and to the northeast, Atzacoalco, "in the house of the herons," which became the site where the missionaries built the church of San Sebastian.

The two most important places in the capital were the sacred precinct of the main temple, with its related temples, schools and other structures (in all, it contained seventy-eight buildings), and the huge plaza in Tlatelolco that served as the principal market place, offering an astonishing variety of products from far and near. The walled precinct of the main temple formed a great square measuring approximately five hundred yards on each side. Today nothing is left of the temple except a few remains that can be seen near the eastern walls of the Cathedral of Mexico. A model of the precinct has recently been installed there.

The palace of Axayacatl, who ruled from 1469 to 1481, stood on the western side of the main temple, and it was here that the

Spaniards were lodged when they arrived in the city as Motecuh-zoma's guests. The palace of Motecuhzoma, facing a broad plaza, stood on the site now occupied by the National Palace of Mexico. And in addition to these and other structures, there was a large number of lesser temples and stone and mortar buildings reserved as living quarters for the nobles, merchants, artists and other persons. The streets of Tenochtitlan were comparatively narrow, many of them with canals through which canoes from the lakeshore could reach the center of the city. The capital boasted many other attractions, and the Spaniards were particularly impressed by the botanical and zoological gardens, as nothing of the kind existed at that time in their native land.

The population of Tenochtitlan at the time of the Conquest has been the subject of considerable controversy, but beyond question it must have amounted at least to a quarter of a million. The activities were many and colorful. Fiestas, sacrifices and other rituals were celebrated in honor of the gods. Teachers and students met in the various *calmecac* and *telpuchcalli*, the pre-Hispanic centers of education. The coming and going of merchant canoes and the constant bustle in the Tlatelolco market impressed the Spaniards so much that they compared the city to an enormous anthill. The military exercises and the arrival and departure of the warriors were other colorful spectacles. In brief, the life of Tenochtitlan was that of a true metropolis. The city was visited by governors and ambassadors from distant regions. Gold, silver, rich feathers, cocoa, bark paper and other types of tribute, along with slaves and victims for the human sacrifices, streamed in along the streets and canals. The Spaniards were right: Tenochtitlan was indeed an anthill, in which each individual worked unceasingly to honor the gods and augment the grandeur of the city.

The Aztec Empire

The wealth and military power of Tenochtitlan were a result of the conquests accomplished by Itzcoatl, who ruled between

1428 and 1440. He had joined with Nezahualcoyotl, king of Tezcoco, to defeat Azcapotzalco and to form the so-called "triple alliance," made up of Tenochtitlan, Tezcoco and the relatively insignificant city of Tlacopan (Tacuba).

Another important factor in the growth of Aztec power was the shrewd work of the royal counselor Tlacaelel, nephew to Itzcoatl, who instituted a number of significant reforms in the tribe's political, religious, social and economic structure. As a profound student of the cultural elements inherited from the Toltecs, he made use of everything that served his purpose—but he also gave everything a special slant, for his purpose was to consolidate the strength and wealth of the city. One of the indigenous texts in the *Codice Matritense* describes how Itzcoatl and Tlacaelel rewarded the principal Aztec chieftains with lands and titles after the victory over Azcapotzalco, and then says that the king and his adviser decided to give their people a new version of Aztec history.

> They preserved an account of their history,
> but later it was burned,
> during the reign of Itzcoatl.
> The lords of Mexico decreed it,
> the lords of Mexico declared:
> "It is not fitting that our people
> should know these pictures.
> Our people, our subjects, will be lost
> and our land destroyed,
> for these pictures are full of lies. . . .

In the new version, recorded in a number of extant documents, the Aztecs claim to be descended from the Toltec nobility, and their gods—Huitzilopochtli in particular—are raised to the same level as the ancient creative gods Tezcatlipoca and Quetzalcoatl. But most important of all is the exalted praise given to what can only be called a mystical conception of warfare, dedicating the Aztec people, the "people of the sun," to the conquest of all other nations. In part the motive was simply to extend the rule of Tenochtitlan, but the major purpose was to capture victims for sacrifice, because the source of all life, the sun, would die unless it were fed with human blood.

As a result, Huitzilopochtli ceased to be the tutelary god of a poor band of outcasts, and his rise to greatness coincided with that of the Aztecs themselves. The old Toltec prayers, most of them directed to Quetzalcoatl, were revised in his favor, and his priests composed a number of others. Since he was identified with the sun, he was called "the Giver of Life" and "the Preserver of Life." Tlacaelel did not originate the idea that Huitzilopochtli-the-Sun had to be fed the most precious food of all—human blood—but he was unquestionably responsible for the central importance that this idea acquired in the Aztec religion.

There is good evidence that human sacrifices were performed in the Valley of Mexico before the arrival of the Aztecs, but apparently no other tribe ever performed them with such frequency. The explanation seems to be that Tlacaelel persuaded the Aztec kings (he was counselor to Motecuhzoma I and his successor Axayacatl after the death of Itzcoatl) that their mission was to extend the dominions of Huitzilopochtli so that there would be a constant supply of captives to be sacrificed. Fray Diego de Duran wrote that Itzcoatl "took only those actions which were counseled by Tlacaelel," and that he believed it was his mission "to gather together all the nations" in the service of his god. It was also Tlacaelel who suggested the building of the great main temple in Tenochtitlan, dedicated to Huitzilopochtli. Before the Spaniards destroyed it, it was the scene of innumerable sacrifices of captives, first from nearby places and later from such distant regions as Oaxaca, Chiapas and Guatemala.

The changes brought about by Tlacaelel in Aztec religious thought and ritual were his most important accomplishments, but he also reformed the judicial system, the army, the protocol of the royal court and the organization of *pochtecas*, or traveling merchants, and he even directed the creation of a large botanical garden in Oaxtepec, on the outskirts of Cuauhtla in the present-day state of Morelos. Despite his key role in Aztec history, Tlacaelel never consented to become king, even though the nobles offered him the throne on the death of Itzcoatl in 1440 and again on the death of Motecuhzoma I in 1469. He preferred to be the "power behind the throne," using his influence to realize what he considered to be the grand destiny of his people. He died a little before 1481, without suspecting, of course, that the magnificence and power for which he was so largely responsible would be destroyed in less than forty years. Considering the unquestionable brilliance of this unusual man, who has been seriously neglected by the historians, one is tempted to ask: What would have happened had the Spaniards arrived during his lifetime? The question is unanswerable, but at least it is an interesting topic for speculation.

To return for a moment to the conquests inspired by Tlacaelel's advice, they began, as we have seen, with the defeat of Azcapotzalco and the formation of the alliance with Tezcoco and Tlacopan. Then the Aztecs set out to conquer the other city-states around the lake, and one by one Coyoacan, Cuitlahuac, Xochimilco and Chalco were forced to submit. Other states, alarmed by the Aztecs' growing power, elected to sign treaties with Tenochtitlan and to deliver it tribute. Among these was the city-state of the Tlahuicas, a people with the same language and culture as the Aztecs, in the southern part of what is now the state of Morelos.

Next the Aztecs marched eastward toward the Gulf coast, where the people of Cempoala also agreed to pay tribute. It was in Cempoala that the Spaniards later took excellent advantage of the enmity the Cempoaltecas bore toward their masters.

The succeeding phase of Aztec expansion was toward the south. Sometimes the armies arrived as conquerors, at other times in search of trade, but their constant aim was to increase the power of Tenochtitlan. They dominated the present-day states of Oaxaca and Chiapas, penetrated into Guatemala and even—according to some accounts—reached the Isthmus of Panama, sending or bringing back tribute and trade goods to their capital.

The Aztecs, however, always respected the independence of

their neighbors, the Tlaxcaltecas, whose state was a "confederation of four republics." There is no doubt that Tenochtitlan could have overwhelmed Tlaxcala without too much difficulty, and the reason it did not is probably that it wanted a nearby source of victims for the human sacrifices. Therefore the Aztecs maintained an almost perpetual state of war with Tlaxcala, but never actually conquered it. Also, the Aztecs seem to have regarded the frequent battles as a convenient way of testing and training their younger warriors. This situation was so hateful to the Tlaxcaltecas that when Cortes arrived they became his most loyal native allies, in the hope that with the aid of the strangers they could at last defeat their oppressors.

By 1519 the Aztecs ruled over several million human beings, who spoke a variety of languages. Their empire stretched from the Pacific Ocean to the Gulf coast and from central Mexico to the present-day Republic of Guatemala. The swift growth of their wealth and power naturally resulted in significant changes in their old way of life. The incipient social classes were consolidated, and the social-political structure became so elaborate that the Spanish conquistadors found it almost as astonishing as some of the city's architectural wonders.

Aztec Society

The stratification into social classes of what had been a mere band of nomads developed in a rather unusual way. Once the Aztecs made contact with the advanced peoples who had inherited Toltec culture, they acquired a profound admiration for them and wanted to link themselves to the Toltec world by bonds of kinship. Hence, they chose as their first king, or *tlatoani*, a nobleman of Toltec origin named Acamapichtli from Culhuacan. He fathered a great many children by various Aztec women, and his descendants formed the nucleus of the social class of nobles, or *pipiltin*, which increased rapidly both in size and importance. The *pipiltin* received a much fuller education than other persons, were allowed to own land in their own names and filled the most important posts in government; the king, or *tlatoani*, could be chosen only from their ranks.

The ordinary citizens formed the social class of the *macehualtin*. They were divided into what have been called geographical clans, that is, groups of related families living in specific localities and making communal use of the land assigned to them. Like the *pipiltin*, the *macehualtin* were required to attend the communal schools, but they were not taught reading, writing, astrology, theology or the other cultural legacies of the Toltecs. They were trained in agriculture and warfare, and some of them became members of the artisan and merchant guilds.

In addition to these two major classes, there were also the *mayeques*, who worked the land for others as slaves or serfs (though almost always for a limited period of time), and a considerable number of actual slaves. It is necessary to point out that neither the *mayeques* nor the slaves were clearly distinguished from the *macehualtin* as social classes.

In Tenochtitlan, Tezcoco and other cities there were groups of wise men known as *tlamatinime*. These scholars carried on the study of the ancient religious thinking of the Toltecs, which Tlacaelel had transformed into a mystical exaltation of war. Despite the popularity of the cult of the war-god, Huitzilopochtli, the *tlamatinime* preserved the old belief in a single supreme god, who was known under a variety of names. Sometimes he was called Tloque-Nahuaque, "Lord of the Close Vicinity," sometimes Ipalnemohuani, "Giver of Life," sometimes Moyocoyatzin, "He who Creates Himself." He also had two aspects, one masculine and one feminine. Thus he was also invoked as Ometeotl, "God of Duality," or given the double names Ometecuhtli and Omecihuatl, "Lord and Lady of Duality," Mictlantecuhtli and Mictecacihuatl, "Lord and Lady of the Region of Death," and others.

It is quite clear that to the *tlamatinime* the long list of names was merely a set of titles for a single god, but the people believed it referred to a whole pantheon of separate deities. This, along with the addition of tutelary gods like Huitzilopochtli, caused the Spaniards to regard the Aztecs as an incredibly idolatrous and polytheistic nation. But a closer analysis of the religious thought of the *tlamatinime* reveals that at least on the upper social levels, only one god was worshiped in Tenochtitlan: the Lord of Duality, the Giver of Life.

Warfare in Ancient Mexico

After Tlacaelel inculcated the idea that Huitzilopochtli-the-Sun had to be fed with the blood of human sacrifices, war became a cultural institution of primary importance in Aztec life, since war was the means of obtaining victims to appease the god's insatiable hunger. Regardless of the ostensible purpose of a military campaign—to conquer new territory, punish a rebellious vassal state, or repel an aggressor—the Aztec warriors never forgot that their first duty was to take captives to be sacrificed. This religious conception of warfare motivated the expansion of the Aztec empire, but it also contributed to its destruction by the Spaniards. On several occasions the Aztecs probably could have wiped out the Spaniards to the last man—their best chance of all was on the Night of Sorrows—but the ceremonial elements in their attitude toward war prevented them from taking full advantage of their opportunities.

As in other cities in central Mexico, military training in Tenochtitlan began during early youth. The army was made up of squads of twenty men, which were combined to form larger units of about four hundred, under a *tiachcauh* who came from the same clan as the warriors he commanded. The more important leaders were usually Eagle or Jaguar Knights, with such titles as *tlacatecatl* (chief of men) and *tlacochcalcatl* (chief of the house of arrows).

The most important offensive weapon of the Aztecs was the *macana*, a sort of paddle-shaped wooden club edged with sharp bits of obsidian. It was so awesomely effective that on more than one occasion during the Conquest warriors beheaded Spanish horses at a single stroke. Other widely used arms were the *atlatl*, or spear thrower, bows and arrows of different sizes, blowguns and a variety of spears and lances, most of them with obsidian points. The defensive weapons were shields made of wood or woven fibers—often elaborately painted and adorned with feathers—and quilted cotton armor. Some of the warriors also wore various types of masks and headdresses to show that they were Eagle or Jaguar Knights or belonged to the higher military ranks.

A war or battle always commenced with a certain ritual: shields, arrows and cloaks of a special kind were sent to the enemy leaders as a formal declaration that they would soon be attacked. This explains the Aztecs' surprise when the Spaniards, their guests, suddenly turned on them without any apparent motive and—more important—without the customary ritual warning.

Pre-Hispanic Education

For over a hundred years before the Conquest, education in Tenochtitlan was compulsory for all male children. They studied either in the specialized *calmecac*, of which there were at least six in the city, or the *telpochcalli*, which were attended by the great majority. The students in the *calmecac* were taught to read and interpret the codices and calendars; they also studied the tribe's history and traditions, and memorized the sacred hymns and other texts. So much emphasis was placed on accurate memorization that after the Conquest it was possible to record many poems and traditions that would otherwise have been lost forever. Most of the students in the *calmecac* were sons of nobles or priests, but there is evidence that children of humble origin were sometimes admitted if they showed exceptional aptitude.

Almost every sector or clan in Tenochtitlan had its own *telpochcalli*, dedicated to the god Tezcatlipoca. The students were taught the fundamentals of religion and ethics, and were also trained in the arts of war. In comparison with the *calmecac*, the *telpochcalli* offered a more basic and practical education. As we have said, every boy had to attend one of these two types of schools, and every father had to make a solemn vow, on the birth of a son, that he would send the boy to school when he reached the proper age, which seems to have fluctuated between six and nine years.

Pre-Hispanic Writing and Calendars

The highest cultures in ancient Mexico—especially the Mayas, Mixtecs, Toltecs and Aztecs—succeeded in developing their own systems of writing, as we can see from their carved inscriptions and the few pre-Columbian codices that have been preserved. The Aztec system was a combination of pictographic, ideographic and partially phonetic characters or glyphs, representing numerals, calendar signs, names of persons, place names, etc. The Aztecs came closest to true phonetic writing in their glyphs for place names, some of which contained phonetic analyses of syllables or even of letters. For example, the sounds *a*, *e* and *o* were indicated by the symbols for water (*atl*), bean (*etl*) and road (*otli*). The paper used in the codices was made by pounding and burnishing strips of bark from the amate tree (*ficus petiolaris*). The illustrations in the present book have been adapted from post-Hispanic codices, of course, but the original artists used the old modes to depict their version of the Conquest.

Like the Mixtecs and Mayas, the Aztecs had two principal types of calendars. One was the *xiupohualli,* or "year-count," based on the astronomical year and made up of eighteen groups or months of twenty days each, with a remaining period of five days, called *nemontemi,* "those who are there," that was considered extremely unlucky. Despite the additional five days at the end, it became obvious that the calendar was moving ahead of the actual year, and therefore an extra day was added to every fourth year, as with our leap year. The other form of calendar was the *tonalpohualli,* or "day-count." It was not based on the astronomical year, for its twenty months had only thirteen days each; instead it was calibrated to a fifty-two-year "century." The *xiupohualli* and *tonalpohualli* were related in various ways, but the whole topic of pre-Hispanic calendars is far too complicated to be explained in a brief space. We have kept a few of the Aztec year, month and day names in this book, with explanatory footnotes where needed.

Indigenous Literature

The literary "remains" that have survived the Conquest and the intervening years are not as well known as the sculpture and architecture of ancient Mexico, but they are surprisingly rich and abundant. As we have seen, the Aztecs, Mayas and other peoples had their own modes of writing, and some of the pre-Conquest codices are still in existence. In addition, the system of memorization employed in the *calmecac* and *telpochcalli* preserved many of the ancient hymns, myths, epic narratives and other literary compositions. It is true that the Spanish conquistadors – along with certain churchmen – burned almost all of the codices and destroyed the pre-Hispanic centers of education. But a few remarkable missionaries, particularly Bernardino de Sahagun and Diego de Duran, undertook to gather up whatever they could of indigenous literature. They managed to acquire a few codices that had escaped the flames, but their major accomplishment was to save a great many of the old songs and narratives that were still faithfully remembered after the Conquest. They worked out means of writing the native languages with the Latin alphabet, and this enabled them—and their Indian pupils—to record the texts in the original words.

Dr. Angel Maria Garibay K., the most important modern authority on pre-Hispanic literature, has shown that more than forty manuscripts containing Aztec literature are extant in various European and American libraries. They offer a broad range of literary types: religious, lyric, epic and dramatic poetry, and prose history, legends, moral teachings, etc. Some of them also present poems and prose narratives describing the Conquest, written or dictated in Nahuatl by persons who witnessed that tragic drama with their own eyes, and the major part of this book is made up of selections from these indigenous accounts. The Appendix gives a brief description of the main sources from which we have drawn.

Pronunciation of Nahuatl Words

The Nahuatl language, which is also known as Aztec or Mexican, is part of the great Uto-Aztec linguistic family. It has been spoken in central and southern Mexico, as well as in various parts of Central America, from Toltec times to the present.

Written Nahuatl, using the Latin alphabet, was introduced by the Spanish missionaries soon after the Conquest. With the exception of *x*, which is pronounced like the English *sh*, the letters have the same phonetic value as in Spanish.

Practically all Nahuatl words are accented on the next to last syllable. This is often indicated today by accents used according to rules of Spanish accentuation.

Conclusion

There were a great many other institutions and customs in ancient Mexico in addition to those we have described, of course, and many of them are relevant to the story of the Conquest in one way or another. But it is obviously impossible to describe the whole panorama of Aztec life within the limits of an Introduction. Therefore the reader interested in acquiring a more detailed knowledge of pre-Hispanic history and culture, or in comparing the native accounts of the Conquest with those of the Spaniards or of later historians, is referred to the Selected Bibliography.

We wish to express our profound gratitude to Dr. Angel Maria Garibay K., director of the Seminary of Nahuatl Culture at the University of Mexico, for his generosity in permitting us to make unrestricted use of his Spanish translations of many Nahuatl texts. We are also grateful to Alberto Beltran for the many pen-and-ink drawings that illustrate this book. They are faithful representations of the indigenous originals.

Finally, we wish to make it clear that this book is not a critical edition of the native texts. We have prepared it for the general reader, and although we could not avoid the use of footnotes, we have tried to keep them to a minimum. Our greatest hope is that this modest work will create further interest in the native accounts of the Conquest. A calm examination of the encounter between two worlds, the Indian and the Spanish, from whose dramatic union Mexico and Latin America in general are descended, will help us to understand one of the most profound sources of the conflicts, grandeurs and miseries of that large portion of our hemisphere.

MIGUEL LEON-PORTILLA

*Instituto Indigenista
Interamericano,
Mexico City*

[1] The Spaniards spelled his name Montezuma. In present-day Mexico it is usually spelled Moctezuma.

[2] In Nahuatl symbolism, the juxtaposition of these two colors signified wisdom.

[3] A quilted cotton tunic soaked in brine. The Spaniards adopted it from the Indians because it was superior to their own armor in hot weather.

[4] The name of several different plants used as soap.

[5] Bernal Diaz del Castillo, *The Discovery and Conquest of Mexico* (New York: Farrar, Straus and Cudahy; paper, Grove Press, 1956), pp. 218-219.

Broken spears lie in the roads;
we have torn our hair in our grief.
The houses are roofless now, and their walls
are red with blood . . .

ELEGY FOR TENOCHTITLAN

The Broken Spears

Chapter One

Omens Foretelling
the Arrival of the Spaniards

Introduction

The documents presented in the first thirteen chapters relate the events that began a few years before the arrival of the Spaniards on the east coast of Mexico and ended with the fall of Tenochtitlan to the conquistadors. The last two chapters offer, by way of conclusion, a somewhat different account of the Conquest written in 1528 by the anonymous informants of Tlatelolco, and three of the *icnocuicatl* (threnodies, or songs of sorrow) lamenting the defeat and destruction of the Aztec capital.

The texts have been arranged to give a chronological narrative of the Conquest, and they contain a number of obvious discrepancies and contradictions. We have not attempted to solve all of the problems which these discrepancies pose for the historian. Our fundamental concern is with the human interest of the accounts, which reveal how the Nahuas interpreted the downfall of their civilization.

This first chapter begins with a passage from the *Codex Florentino;* the original text is in the Nahuatl of Sahagun's native informants. It is followed by two selections from the *Historia de Tlaxcala* by Diego Munoz Camargo, who married into the nobility of Tlaxcala. The Tlaxcaltecas allied themselves with Cortes, and Munoz Camargo wrote from their point of view, but his description of the omens which appeared in Mexico agrees quite closely with that of Sahagun's informants.

The Omens as Described by Sahagun's Informants

The first bad omen: Ten years before the Spaniards first came here, a bad omen appeared in the sky. It was like a flaming ear of corn, or a fiery signal, or the blaze of daybreak; it seemed to bleed fire, drop by drop, like a wound in the sky. It was wide at the base and narrow at the peak, and it shone in the very heart of the heavens.

This is how it appeared: it shone in the eastern sky in the middle of the night. It appeared at midnight and burned till the break of day, but it vanished at the rising of the sun. The time during which it appeared to us was a full year, beginning in the year 12-House.

When it first appeared, there was great outcry and confusion. The people clapped their hands against their mouths; they were amazed and frightened, and asked themselves what it could mean.

The second bad omen: The temple of Huitzilopochtli[1]

burst into flames. It is thought that no one set it afire, that it burned down of its own accord. The name of its divine site was Tlacateccan [House of Authority].

And now it is burning, the wooden columns are burning! The flames, the tongues of fire shoot out, the bursts of fire shoot up into the sky! The flames swiftly destroyed all the woodwork of the temple. When the fire was first seen, the people shouted: "Mexicanos, come running! We can put it out! Bring your water jars...!" But when they threw water on the blaze it only flamed higher. They could not put it out, and the temple burned to the ground.

The third bad omen: A temple was damaged by a lightning-bolt. This was the temple of Xiuhtecuhtli,[2] which was built of straw, in the place known as Tzonmolco.[3] It was raining that day, but it was only a light rain or a drizzle, and no thunder was heard. Therefore the lightning-bolt was taken as an omen. The people said: "The temple was struck by a blow from the sun."

The fourth bad omen: Fire streamed through the sky while the sun was still shining. It was divided into three parts. It flashed out from where the sun sets and raced straight to where the sun rises, giving off a shower of sparks like a red-hot coal. When the people saw its long train streaming through the heavens, there was a great outcry and confusion, as if they were shaking a thousand little bells.

The fifth bad omen: The wind lashed the water until it boiled. It was as if it were boiling with rage, as if it were shattering itself in its frenzy. It began from far off, rose high in the air and dashed against the walls of the houses. The flooded houses collapsed into the water. This was in the lake that is next to us.

five

The sixth bad omen: The people heard a weeping woman night after night. She passed by in the middle of the night, wailing and crying out in a loud voice: "My children, we must flee far away from this city!" At other times she cried: "My children, where shall I take you?"[4]

The seventh bad omen: A strange creature was captured in the nets. The men who fish the lakes caught a bird the color of ashes, a bird resembling a crane. They brought it to Motecuhzoma in the Black House.[5]

This bird wore a strange mirror in the crown of its head. The mirror was pierced in the center like a spindle whorl, and the night sky could be seen in its face. The hour was noon, but the stars and the *mamalhuaztli*[6] could be seen in the face of that mirror. Motecuhzoma took it as a great and bad omen when he saw the stars and the *mamalhuaztli*.

But when he looked at the mirror a second time, he saw a distant plain. People were moving across it, spread out in ranks and coming forward in great haste. They made war against each other and rode on the backs of animals resembling deer.

Motecuhzoma called for his magicians and wise men and asked them: "Can you explain what I have seen? Creatures like human beings, running and fighting ...!" But when they looked into the mirror to answer him, all had vanished away, and they saw nothing.

The eighth bad omen: Monstrous beings appeared in the streets of the city: deformed men with two heads but only one body. They were taken to the Black House and shown to Motecuhzoma; but the moment he saw them, they all vanished away.

The Omens as Described by Munoz Camargo[7]

Ten years before the Spaniards came to this land, the people saw a strange wonder and took it to be an evil sign and portent. This wonder was a great column of flame which burned in the night, shooting out such brilliant sparks and flashes that it seemed to rain fire on the earth and to blaze like daybreak. It seemed to be fastened against the sky in the shape of a pyramid, its base set against the ground, where it was of vast width, and its bulk narrowing to a peak that reached up and touched the heavens. It appeared at midnight and could still be seen at dawn, but in the daytime it was quelled by the force and brilliance of the sun. This portent burned for a year, beginning in the year which the natives called 12-House—that is, 1517 in our Spanish reckoning.

When this sign and portent was first seen, the natives were overcome with terror, weeping and shouting and crying out, and beating the palms of their hands against their mouths, as is their custom. These shouts and cries were accompanied by sacrifices of blood and of human beings, for this was their practice whenever they thought they were endangered by some calamity.

This great marvel caused so much dread and wonder that they spoke of it constantly, trying to imagine what such a strange novelty could signify. They begged the seers and magicians to interpret its meaning, because no such thing had ever been seen or reported anywhere in the world. It should be noted that these signs began to appear ten years before the coming of the Spaniards, but that the year called 12-House in their reckoning was the year 1517, two years before the Spaniards reached this land.

Evil Omens (Codex Florentino)

eight

The second wonder, sign or omen which the natives beheld was this: the temple of the demon Huitzilopochtli, in the sector named Tlacateco, caught fire and burned, though no one had set it afire. The blaze was so great and sudden that wings of flame rushed out of the doors and seemed to touch the sky. When this occurred, there was great confusion and much loud shouting and wailing. The people cried: "Mexicanos! Come as quickly as you can! Bring your water jars to put it out!" Everyone within hearing ran to help, but when they threw water on the fire, it leaped up with even greater violence, and thus the whole temple burned down.

The third wonder and sign was this: a lightning-bolt fell on a temple of idolatry whose roof was made of straw. The name of this temple was Tzonmolco, and it was dedicated to their idol Xiuhtecuhtli. The bolt fell on the temple with neither flash nor thunder, when there was only a light rain, like a dew. It was taken as an omen and miracle which boded evil, and all burned down.

The fourth wonder was this: comets flashed through the sky in the daytime while the sun was shining. They raced by threes from the west to the east with great haste and violence, shooting off bright coals and sparks of fire, and trailing such long tails that their splendor filled the sky. When these portents were seen, the people were terrified, wailing and crying aloud.

The fifth wonder was this: the Lake of Mexico rose when there was no wind. It boiled, and boiled again, and foamed until it reached a great height, until it washed against half the houses in the city. House after house collapsed and was destroyed by the waters.

The sixth wonder was this: the people heard in the night the voice of a weeping woman, who sobbed and sighed and drowned herself in her tears. This woman cried: "O my sons, we are lost ...!" Or she cried: "O my sons, where can I hide you ...?"

The seventh wonder was this: the men whose work is in the Lake of Mexico—the fishermen and other boatmen, or the fowlers in their canoes—trapped a dark-feathered bird resembling a crane and took it to Motecuhzoma so that he might see it. He was in the palace of the Black Hall; the sun was already in the west. This bird was so unique and marvelous that no one could exaggerate its strangeness or describe it well. A round diadem was set in its head in the form of a clear and transparent mirror, in which could be seen the heavens, the three stars in Taurus and the stars in the sign of the Gemini. When Motecuhzoma saw this, he was filled with dread and wonder, for he believed it was a bad omen to see the stars of heaven in the diadem of that bird.

When Motecuhzoma looked into the mirror a second time, he saw a host of people, all armed like warriors, coming forward in well-ordered ranks. They skirmished and fought with each other, and were accompanied by strange deer and other creatures.

Therefore, he called for his magicians and fortune-tellers, whose wisdom he trusted, and asked them what these unnatural visions meant: "My dear and learned friends, I have witnessed great signs in the diadem of a bird, which was brought to me as something new and marvelous that had never been seen before. What I witnessed in that diadem, which is pellucid like a mirror, was a strange host of people rushing toward me across a plain. Now look yourselves, and see what I have seen."

But when they wished to advise their lord on what seemed to them so wondrous a thing, and to give him their judgments, divinations and predictions, the bird suddenly disappeared; and thus they could not offer him any sure opinion.

The eighth wonder and sign that appeared in Mexico: the natives saw two men merged into one body—these they called *tlacantzolli* ("men-squeezed-together")—and others who had two heads but only one body. They were brought to the palace of the Black Hall to be shown to the great Motecuhzoma, but they vanished as soon as he had seen them, and all these signs and others became invisible. To the natives, these marvels augured their death and ruin, signifying that the end of the world was coming and that other peoples would be created to inhabit the earth. They were so frightened and grief-stricken that they could form no judgment about these things, so new and strange and never before seen or reported.

The Wonders and Signs Observed in Tlaxcala

Other signs appeared here in this province of Tlaxcala, a little before the arrival of the Spaniards. The first sign was a radiance that shone in the east every morning three hours before sunrise. This radiance was in the form of a brilliant white cloud which rose to the sky, and the people were filled with dread and wonder, not knowing what it could be.

They also saw another marvelous sign: a whirlwind of dust that rose like a sleeve from the top of the Matlalcueye, now called the Sierra de Tlaxcala.[8] This sleeve rose so high that it seemed to touch the sky. The sign appeared many times throughout a whole year and caused the people great dread and wonder, emotions which are contrary to their bent and to that of their nation. They could only believe that the gods had descended from heaven, and the news flew through the province to the smallest villages. But however this may have been, the arrival of a strange new people was at last reported and confirmed, especially in Mexico, the head of this empire and monarchy.

[1] Sun god and god of war.
[2] Fire god.
[3] Part of the main temple of Tenochtitlan.
[4] Apparently a reference to Cihuacoatl, an ancient earth goddess, who wept and cried out in the night. She is one of the antecedents of the *llorona* (weeping woman), who is still heard in rural Mexico.
[5] The house of magical studies. Motecuhzoma, the king, was a devoted amateur wizard.
[6] Three stars in the constellation Taurus. They were extremely important in the Nahuatl religion: the Nahuas performed various ceremonies in their honor and offered them copal incense three times each night.
[7] This selection from the *Historia de Tlaxcala* obviously is based on the account by Sahagun's informants.
[8] Its present name is La Malinche.

Chapter Two

First Reports of the Spaniards' Arrival

Introduction

The *Cronica mexicana*[1] by Fernando Alvarado Tezozomoc
relates how Motecuhzoma consulted various seers and magicians to
learn whether the omens meant an approaching war or some other
crisis. They could not give him a satisfactory answer. However,
a poor *macehual* (common man) arrived shortly afterward from
the Gulf coast, bringing the first word of the appearance of "towers
or small mountains floating on the waves of the sea." A later
report said that the mountains bore a strange people who "have
very light skin, much lighter than ours. They all have long beards,
and their hair comes only to their ears."

Motecuhzoma was even more distressed by this news than
he had been by the omens. Therefore, he sent messengers and gifts
to the strangers, believing that they might be Quetzalcoatl[2] and

other divinities returning to Mexico, as the codices and traditions promised they would.

Motecuhzoma Questions the Magicians

Motecuhzoma summoned the chief officials of all the villages. He told them to search their villages for magicians and to bring him any they found. The officials returned with a number of these wizards, who were announced and then brought in to the king's presence. They knelt before him, with one knee on the floor, and did him the greatest reverence. He asked them: "Have you not seen strange omens in the sky or on the earth? In the caves under the earth, or in the lakes and streams? A weeping woman, or strange men? Visions, or phantasms, or other such things?"

But the magicians had not seen any of the omens that Motecuhzoma sought to understand, and therefore could not advise him. He said to his *petlacalcatl* [head steward]: "Take these villains away, and lock them up in the Cuauhcalco prison. They shall tell me against their will." The next day he called for his *petlacalcatl* and said to him: "Tell the magicians to say what they believe: whether sickness is going to strike, or hunger, or locusts, or storms on the lake, or droughts, and whether it will rain or not. If war is threatening Mexico, or if there will be sudden deaths, or deaths caused by wild beasts, they are not to hide it from me. They must also tell me if they have heard the voice of Cihuacoatl,[3] for when something is to happen, she is the first to predict it, even long before it takes place."

The magicians answered: "What can we say? The future has already been determined and decreed in heaven, and Motecuhzoma will behold and suffer a great mystery which must come to pass in his land. If our king wishes to know more about it, he will know soon enough, for it comes swiftly. This is what we predict, since he demands that we speak, and since it must surely take place, he can only wait for it."

The *petlacalcatl* returned to Motecuhzoma and told him openly what they had said, that what was to come would come swiftly. Motecuhzoma was astonished to find that this agreed with the prediction made by Nezahualpilli, king of Tezcoco.[4] He said to the *petlacalcatl*: "Question them again about this mystery. Ask them if it will come from the sky or the earth, and from what direction or place it will come, and when this will happen."

The *petlacalcatl* went back to the prison to question them, but when he entered and unlocked the doors, he was terrified to discover that they were not there. He returned to Motecuhzoma and said to him: "My lord, command that I be cut to pieces, or whatever else you wish: for you must know, my lord, that when I arrived and opened the doors, no one was there. I have special guards at the prison, trustworthy men who have served me for years, but none of them heard them escape. I myself believe that they flew away, for they know how to make themselves invisible, which they do every night, and can fly to the ends of the earth. This is what they must have done."

Motecuhzoma said: "Let the villains go. Call the chiefs together, and tell them to go to the villages where the magicians live. Tell them to kill their wives and all their children, and to destroy their houses." He also ordered many servants to go with them to ransack the houses. When the chiefs arrived, they killed the women by hanging them with ropes, and the children by dashing them to pieces against the walls. Then they tore down the houses and even rooted out their foundations.

fifteen

A Macehual Arrives from the Gulf Coast

A few days later a *macehual* [common man] came to the
city from Mictlancuauhtla. No one had sent him, none of the
officials; he came of his own accord. He went directly to the
palace of Motecuhzoma and said to him: "Our lord and king,
forgive my boldness. I am from Mictlancuauhtla. When I went
to the shores of the great sea, there was a mountain range or
small mountain floating in the midst of the water, and moving
here and there without touching the shore. My lord, we have
never seen the like of this, although we guard the coast and are
always on watch."

Motecuhzoma thanked him and said: "You may rest now."
The man who brought this news had no ears, for they had been
cut off, and no toes, for they had also been cut off.

Motecuhzoma said to his *petlacalcatl*: "Take him to the
prison, and guard him well." Then he called for a *teuctlama-
cazqui* [priest] and appointed him his grand emissary. He said
to him: "Go to Cuetlaxtlan, and tell the official in charge of the
village that it is true, strange things have appeared on the great
sea. Tell him to investigate these things himself, so as to learn
what they may signify. Tell him to do this as quickly as he can,
and take the ambassador Cuitlalpitoc with you."

When they arrived in Cuetlaxtlan, the envoys spoke with
the official in charge there, a man named Pinotl. He listened to
them with great attention and then said: "My lords, rest here
with me, and send your attendants out to the shore." The attendants went out and came back in great haste to report that
it was true: they had seen two towers or small mountains
floating on the waves of the sea. The grand emissary said to
Pinotl: "I wish to see these things in person, in order to learn
what they are, for I must testify to our lord as an eyewitness. I

will be satisfied with this and will report to him exactly what I see." Therefore he went out to the shore with Cuitlalpitoc, and they saw what was floating there, beyond the edge of the water. They also saw that seven or eight of the strangers had left it in a small boat and were fishing with hooks and lines.

The grand emissary and Cuitlalpitoc climbed up into a broad-limbed tree. From there they saw how the strangers were catching fish and how, when they were done, they returned to the ship in their small boat. The grand emissary said: "Come, Cuitlalpitoc." They climbed down from the tree and went back to the village, where they took hasty leave of Pinotl. They returned as swiftly as possible to the great city of Tenochtitlan, to report to Motecuhzoma what they had observed.

When they reached the city, they went directly to the king's palace and spoke to him with all due reverence and humility: "Our lord and king, it is true that strange people have come to the shores of the great sea. They were fishing from a small boat, some with rods and others with a net. They fished until late and then they went back to their two great towers and climbed up into them. There were about fifteen of these people, some with blue jackets, others with red, others with black or green, and still others with jackets of a soiled color, very ugly, like our *ichtilmatli*.[5] There were also a few without jackets. On their heads they wore red kerchiefs, or bonnets of a fine scarlet color, and some wore large round hats like small *comales*,[6] which must have been sunshades. They have very light skin, much lighter than ours. They all have long beards, and their hair comes only to their ears."

Motecuhzoma was downcast when he heard this report, and did not speak a word.

Preparations Ordered by Motecuhzoma

After a long silence, Motecuhzoma finally spoke: "You are the chiefs of my own house and palace and I can place more faith and credit in you than in anyone else because you have always told me the truth. Go with the *petlacalcatl* and bring me the man who is locked up in the jail, the *macehual* who came as a messenger from the coast." They went to the jail, but when they opened the doors, they could not find him anywhere. They hurried back to tell Motecuhzoma, who was even more astonished and terrified than they were. He said: "It is a natural thing, for almost everyone is a magician. But hear what I tell you now, and if you reveal anything of what I am about to command, I will bury you under my halls, and your wives and children will be killed, and your property seized. Your houses will be destroyed to the bottom of their foundations, until the water seeps up, and your parents and all your kin will be put to death. Now bring me in secret two of the best artists among the silversmiths, and two lapidaries who are skillful at working emeralds."[7]

They went and returned and said to him: "Our lord, here are the craftsmen you commanded us to bring you." Motecuhzoma said: "Tell them to enter." They entered, and he said to them: "Come here to me, my fathers. You are to know that I have called for you to have you make certain objects. But take care that you do not reveal this to anyone, for if you do, it will mean the ruin of your houses to their foundations, and the loss of your goods, and death to yourselves, your wives, your children and your kin, for all shall die. Each of you is to make two objects, and you are to make them in my presence, here in secret in this palace."

He told one craftsman: "Make a throat-band or chain of

gold, with links four fingers wide and very thin, and let each piece and medallion bear rich emeralds in the center and at the sides, like earrings, two by two. Then make a pair of gold bracelets, with chains of gold hanging from them. And do this with all the haste in the world."

He ordered the other craftsman to make two great fans with rich feathers, in the center of one side a half-moon of gold, on the other a gold sun, both well burnished so that they would shine from far away. He also told him to make two gold armlets rich with feathers. And he ordered each of the lapidaries to make two double bracelets—that is, for both wrists and both ankles—of gold set with fine emeralds.

Then he ordered his *petlacalcatl* to bring in secret many *canutos*[8] of gold, and plumage of the noblest sort, and many emeralds and other rich stones of the finest quality. All of this was given to the artisans and in a few days they had finished their work. One morning, after the king had risen, they sent a palace hunchback to the king Motecuhzoma, to beg him to come to their workroom.

When he entered, they showed him great reverence and said: "Our lord, the work is finished. Please inspect it." Motecuhzoma saw that the work was excellent, and he told them that all had been done to his satisfaction and pleasure. He called for his *petlacalcatl* and said: "Give each of these, my grandfathers, a portion of various rich cloths; and huipiles[9] and skirts for my grandmothers; and cotton, chiles, corn, squash seeds and beans, the same amount to each." And with this the craftsmen returned to their homes contented. . . .

[1] Written about 1598; the only surviving text is in Spanish. The same author also wrote the *Cronica mexicayotl* in Nahuatl.
[2] God of learning and of the wind.
[3] The weeping goddess. See Chapter 1, note 4.
[4] Not long before the first omen was seen, Nezahualpilli told Motecuhzoma

that, according to his fortune-tellers, Mexico would soon be ruled by strangers. Motecuhzoma replied that his own fortune-tellers had predicted otherwise. Nezahualpilli then suggested that they settle the matter by playing a series of ritual ball games, with the outcome to decide who was right; he also offered to wager his whole kingdom against three turkey cocks. Motecuhzoma agreed and won the first two games, but Nezahualpilli won the last three in succession.

[5] A cloak made from maguey fibers, worn by fastening a knot at the shoulder.

[6] The *comal*, still used in Mexico, is a wide, flat pottery dish on which *tortillas* are baked.

[7] The Aztecs imported emeralds from the Muzo region of present-day Colombia, in South America, the only source then available.

[8] Small tubes, often quills, in which gold dust was kept.

[9] The *huipil*, still worn in some parts of Mexico, is a woman's long, sleeveless blouse.

twenty

Chapter Three

The Messengers' Journeys

Introduction

The native documents—principally those by Sahagun's informants—describe the various journeys made by Motecuhzoma's messengers to the Gulf coasts where the strangers had appeared. The texts describing the instructions that Motecuhzoma gave to his envoys are presented first. These show clearly how the Nahuas attempted to explain the coming of the Spaniards by a projection of earlier ideas: they assumed that the new arrivals were Quetzalcoatl and other deities.

Then the documents relate how the messengers reached the coast and were received by the Spaniards, to whom they brought gifts from Motecuhzoma. The descriptions of the gifts offered to

twenty-one

Cortes, and of his successful attempt to frighten the messengers by firing an arquebus in front of them, are especially interesting.

The third part of this chapter deals with the messengers' return to Tenochtitlan and the information they brought back to Motecuhzoma about the Spaniards, their firearms, the animals they rode (a species of huge "deer," but without horns), their mastiff dogs and so on.

All the texts in this chapter are from the *Codex Florentino*.

Motecuhzoma Instructs His Messengers

Motecuhzoma then gave orders to Pinotl of Cuetlaxtlan and to other officials. He said to them: "Give out this order: a watch is to be kept along all the shores at Nauhtla, Tuztlan, Mictlancuauhtla, wherever the strangers appear." The officials left at once and gave orders for the watch to be kept.

Motecuhzoma now called his chiefs together: Tlilpotonque, the serpent woman,[1] Cuappiatzin, the chief of the house of arrows,[2] Quetzalaztatzin, the keeper of the chalk,[3] and Hecateupatiltzin, the chief of the refugees from the south. He told them the news that had been brought to him and showed them the objects he had ordered made. He said: "We all admire these blue turquoises, and they must be guarded well. The whole treasure must be guarded well. If anything is lost, your houses will be destroyed and your children killed, even those who are still in the womb."

The year 13-Rabbit now approached its end. And when it was about to end, they appeared, they were seen again. The report of their coming was brought to Motecuhzoma, who immediately sent out messengers. It was as if he thought the new arrival was our prince Quetzalcoatl.

This is what he felt in his heart: *He has appeared! He has come back! He will come here, to the place of his throne and canopy, for that is what he promised when he departed!* Motecuhzoma sent five messengers to greet the strangers and to bring them gifts. They were led by the priest in charge of the sanctuary of Yohualichan. The second was from Tepoztlan; the third, from Tizatlan; the fourth, from Huehuetlan; and the fifth, from Mictlan the Great.[4] He said to them: "Come forward, my Jaguar Knights, come forward. It is said that our lord has returned to this land. Go to meet him. Go to hear him. Listen well to what he tells you; listen and remember."

The Gifts Sent to the New Arrivals

Motecuhzoma also said to the messengers: "Here is what you are to bring our lord. This is the treasure of Quetzalcoatl." This treasure was the god's finery: a serpent mask inlaid with turquoise, a decoration for the breast made of quetzal[5] feathers, a collar woven in the petatillo style[6] with a gold disk in the center, and a shield decorated with gold and mother-of-pearl and bordered with quetzal feathers with a pendant of the same feathers.

There was also a mirror like those which the ritual dancers wore on their buttocks. The reverse of this mirror was a turquoise mosaic: it was encrusted and adorned with turquoises. And there was a spear-thrower inlaid with turquoise, a bracelet of chalchihuites[7] hung with little gold bells and a pair of sandals as black as obsidian.

Motecuhzoma also gave them the finery of Tezcatlipoca.[8] This finery was: a helmet in the shape of a cone, yellow with gold and set with many stars, a number of earrings adorned with little gold bells, a fringed and painted vest with feathers as delicate as foam and a blue cloak known as "the ringing bell," which reached to the ears and was fastened with a knot.

There was also a collar of fine shells to cover the breast. This collar was adorned with the finest snail shells, which seemed to escape from the edges. And there was a mirror to be hung in back, a set of little gold bells and a pair of white sandals.

Then Motecuhzoma gave them the finery of Tlaloc.[9] This finery was: a headdress made of quetzal feathers, as green as if it were growing, with an ornament of gold and mother-of-pearl, earrings in the form of serpents, made of *chalchihuites*, a vest adorned with *chalchihuites* and a collar also of *chalchihuites*, woven in the petatillo style, with a disk of gold.

There was also a serpent wand inlaid with turquoise, a mirror to be hung in back, with little bells, and a cloak bordered with red rings.

Then Motecuhzoma gave them the finery of Quetzalcoatl. This finery was: a diadem made of jaguar skin and pheasant feathers and adorned with a large green stone, round turquoise earrings with curved pendants of shell and gold, a collar of *chalchihuites* in the petatillo style with a disk of gold in the center, a cloak with red borders, and little gold bells for the feet.

There was also a golden shield, pierced in the middle, with quetzal feathers around the rim and a pendant of the same feathers, the crooked staff of Ehecatl[10] with a cluster of white stones at the crook, and his sandals of fine soft rubber.

These were the many kinds of adornments that were known as "divine adornments." They were placed in the possession of the messengers to be taken as gifts of welcome along with many other objects, such as a golden snail shell and a golden diadem. All these objects were packed into great baskets; they were loaded into panniers for the long journey.

Then Motecuhzoma gave the messengers his final orders. He said to them: "Go now, without delay. Do reverence to our lord the god. Say to him: 'Your deputy, Motecuhzoma, has sent us to you. Here are the presents with which he welcomes you home to Mexico.'"

The Messengers Contact the Spaniards

When they arrived at the shore of the sea, they were taken in canoes to Xicalanco. They placed the baskets in the same canoes in which they rode, in order to keep them under their personal vigilance. From Xicalanco they followed the coast until they sighted the ships of the strangers.

When they came up to the ships, the strangers asked them: "Who are you? Where are you from?"

"We have come from the City of Mexico."[11]

The strangers said: "You may have come from there, or you may not have. Perhaps you are only inventing it. Perhaps you are mocking us." But their hearts were convinced; they were satisfied in their hearts. They lowered a hook from the bow of the ship, and then a ladder, and the messengers came aboard.

One by one they did reverence to Cortes by touching the ground before him with their lips. They said to him: "If the god will deign to hear us, your deputy Motecuhzoma has sent us to render you homage. He has the City of Mexico in his care. He says: 'The god is weary.'"

Then they arrayed the Captain in the finery they had brought him as presents. With great care they fastened the turquoise mask in place, the mask of the god with its crossband of quetzal feathers. A golden earring hung down on either side of this mask. They dressed him in the decorated vest and the collar woven in the petatillo style—the collar of *chalchihuites*, with a disk of gold in the center.

Next they fastened the mirror to his hips, dressed him in the cloak known as "the ringing bell" and adorned his feet with the greaves used by the Huastecas,[12] which were set with *chalchihuites* and hung with little gold bells. In his hand they placed the shield with its fringe and pendant of quetzal feathers, its ornaments of gold and mother-of-pearl. Finally they set before him the pair of black sandals. As for the other objects of divine finery, they only laid them out for him to see.

The Captain asked them: "And is this all? Is this your gift of welcome? Is this how you greet people?"

They replied: "This is all, our lord. This is what we have brought you."

Cortes Frightens the Messengers

Then the Captain gave orders, and the messengers were chained by the feet and by the neck. When this had been done, the great cannon was fired off. The messengers lost their senses and fainted away. They fell down side by side and lay where they had fallen. But the Spaniards quickly revived them: they lifted them up, gave them wine to drink and then offered them food.

The Captain said to them: "I have heard that the Mexicans are very great warriors, very brave and terrible. If a Mexican is fighting alone, he knows how to retreat, turn back, rush forward and conquer, even if his opponents are ten or even

The Spaniards and Motecuhzoma's Messengers
(Codex Florentino)

twenty-seven

twenty. But my heart is not convinced. I want to see it for myself. I want to find out if you are truly that strong and brave."

Then he gave them swords, spears and leather shields. He said: "It will take place very early, at daybreak. We are going to fight each other in pairs, and in this way we will learn the truth. We will see who falls to the ground!"

They said to the Captain: "Our lord, we were not sent here for this by your deputy Motecuhzoma! We have come on an exclusive mission, to offer you rest and repose and to bring you presents. What the lord desires is not within our warrant. If we were to do this, it might anger Motecuhzoma, and he would surely put us to death."

The Captain replied: "No, it must take place. I want to see for myself, because even in Castile they say you are famous as brave warriors. Therefore, eat an early meal. I will eat too. Good cheer!"

With these words he sent them away from the ship. They were scarcely into their canoes when they began to paddle furiously. Some of them even paddled with their hands, so fierce was the anxiety burning in their souls. They said to each other: "My captains, paddle with all your might! Faster, faster! Nothing must happen to us here! Nothing must happen . . . !"

They arrived in great haste at Xicalanco, took a hurried meal there, and then pressed on until they came to Tecpant-layacac. From there they rushed ahead and arrived in Cuet-laxtlan. As on the previous journey, they stopped there to rest. When they were about to depart, the village official said to them: "Rest for at least a day! At least catch your breath!"

They said: "No, we must keep on! We must report to our king, Motecuhzoma. We will tell him what we have seen, and it is a terrifying thing. Nothing like it has ever been seen before!" Then they left in great haste and continued to the City of Mexico. They entered the city at night, in the middle of the night.

Motecuhzoma Awaits Word from the Messengers

While the messengers were away, Motecuhzoma could neither sleep nor eat, and no one could speak with him. He thought that everything he did was in vain, and he sighed almost every moment. He was lost in despair, in the deepest gloom and sorrow. Nothing could comfort him, nothing could calm him, nothing could give him any pleasure.

He said: "What will happen to us? Who will outlive it? Ah, in other times I was contented, but now I have death in my heart! My heart burns and suffers, as if it were drowned in spices...! But will our lord come here?"

Then he gave orders to the watchmen, to the men who guarded the palace: "Tell me, even if I am sleeping: 'The messengers have come back from the sea.'" But when they went to tell him, he immediately said: "They are not to report to me here. I will receive them in the House of the Serpent. Tell them to go there." And he gave this order: "Two captives are to be painted with chalk."

The messengers went to the House of the Serpent, and Motecuhzoma arrived. The two captives were then sacrificed before his eyes: their breasts were torn open, and the messengers were sprinkled with their blood. This was done because the messengers had completed a difficult mission: they had seen the gods, their eyes had looked on their faces. They had even conversed with the gods!

The Messengers' Report

When the sacrifice was finished, the messengers reported to the king. They told him how they had made the journey, and what they had seen, and what food the strangers ate. Motecuhzoma was astonished and terrified by their report, and the description of the strangers' food astonished him above all else.

He was also terrified to learn how the cannon roared, how its noise resounded, how it caused one to faint and grow deaf. The messengers told him: "A thing like a ball of stone comes out of its entrails: it comes out shooting sparks and raining fire. The smoke that comes out with it has a pestilent odor, like that of rotten mud. This odor penetrates even to the brain and causes the greatest discomfort. If the cannon is aimed against a mountain, the mountain splits and cracks open. If it is aimed against a tree, it shatters the tree into splinters. This is a most unnatural sight, as if the tree had exploded from within."

The messengers also said: "Their trappings and arms are all made of iron. They dress in iron and wear iron casques on their heads. Their swords are iron; their bows are iron; their shields are iron; their spears are iron. Their deer carry them on their backs wherever they wish to go. These deer, our lord, are as tall as the roof of a house.

"The strangers' bodies are completely covered, so that only their faces can be seen. Their skin is white, as if it were made of lime. They have yellow hair, though some of them have black. Their beards are long and yellow, and their moustaches are also yellow. Their hair is curly, with very fine strands.

"As for their food, it is like human food. It is large and white, and not heavy. It is something like straw, but with the taste of a cornstalk, of the pith of a cornstalk. It is a little sweet, as if it were flavored with honey; it tastes of honey, it is sweet-tasting food.

"Their dogs are enormous, with flat ears and long, dangling tongues. The color of their eyes is a burning yellow; their eyes flash fire and shoot off sparks. Their bellies are hollow, their flanks long and narrow. They are tireless and very powerful. They bound here and there, panting, with their tongues hanging out. And they are spotted like an ocelot."

When Motecuhzoma heard this report, he was filled with terror. It was as if his heart had fainted, as if it had shriveled. It was as if he were conquered by despair.

[1] The king's chief counselor was traditionally given this title, which was the name of an earth goddess with masculine as well as feminine attributes. The word *coatl*, "serpent," also means "twin."

[2] The suffix *-tzin* indicates high rank or influence.

[3] Official in charge of the colors with which the priests painted their bodies before performing certain rituals.

[4] Mitla, in the Oaxaca region.

[5] A tropical bird of Central America.

[6] Like a *petate* (rush mat), but with a finer weave.

[7] Green stones: jade and jadeite.

[8] Chief god of the pantheon, with solar attributes.

[9] God of the rain.

[10] God of the wind, a frequent guise of Quetzalcoatl.

[11] The Spaniards and the messengers could communicate because Cortes had brought with him La Malinche and Jeronimo de Aguilar. La Malinche was a native of the Gulf coast who spoke both Nahuatl and Mayan. She joined the Spaniards (who called her Dona Marina) of her own free will and served them faithfully as interpreter throughout the Conquest. Aguilar was a Spaniard who had been shipwrecked in Yucatan in 1511 during a voyage from Darien to Hispaniola. By the time Cortes ransomed him from the natives eight years later, he spoke Mayan fluently. La Malinche translated the Nahuatl of the messengers into Mayan for Aguilar, who then translated it into Spanish for the conquistadors.

[12] Indians of eastern Mexico.

thirty-one

Chapter Four

Motecuhzoma's Terror and Apathy

Introduction

When Motecuhzoma heard the messengers' report, with its description of strange animals and other marvels, his thoughts were even more disturbed. Sahagun's informants tell us how he sent out his magicians and warlocks in the hope that they could harm the Spaniards with their magic, or at least prevent them from approaching Tenochtitlan. In his uncertainty about the nature of the strangers—he still thought they might be gods—he also sent out captives to be sacrificed in their presence. The informants give us a vivid account of the Spaniards' reactions to this rite.

The magicians failed completely in their attempts either to harm the Spaniards or to drive them away. The messengers reported all this to Motecuhzoma in Tenochtitlan. Both he and his people lived through days of intense fear, because it was now certain that the "gods" intended to march on the Aztec capital. The informants offer what could almost be called a psychological portrait of Motecuhzoma as he struggled with his fears and uncertainties. Finally we see how the grand *tlatoani* (king) resigned himself and waited for the inevitable.

The texts in this chapter are from the *Codex Florentino*.

Motecuhzoma Sends Out Wizards and Magicians

It was at this time that Motecuhzoma sent out a deputation. He sent out his most gifted men, his prophets and wizards, as many as he could gather. He also sent out his noblest and bravest warriors. They had to take their provisions with them on the journey: live hens[1] and hens' eggs and tortillas. They also took whatever the strangers might request, or whatever might please them.

Motecuhzoma also sent captives to be sacrificed, because the strangers might wish to drink their blood. The envoys sacrificed these captives in the presence of the strangers, but when the white men saw this done, they were filled with disgust and loathing. They spat on the ground, or wiped away their tears, or closed their eyes and shook their heads in abhorrence. They refused to eat the food that was sprinkled with blood, because it reeked of it; it sickened them, as if the blood had rotted.

Motecuhzoma ordered the sacrifice because he took the Spaniards to be gods; he believed in them and worshiped them as deities. That is why they were called "Gods who have come from heaven." As for the Negroes,[2] they were called "soiled gods."

Then the strangers ate the tortillas, the eggs and the hens, and fruit of every variety: guavas, avocados, prickly pears and the many other kinds that grow here. There was food for the "deer" also: reed shoots and green grasses.

Motecuhzoma had sent the magicians to learn what sort of people the strangers might be, but they were also to see if they could work some charm against them, or do them some mischief. They might be able to direct a harmful wind against them, or cause them to break out in sores, or injure them in some way. Or they might be able to repeat some enchanted word, over and over, that would cause them to fall sick, or die, or return to their own land.

The magicians carried out their mission against the Spaniards, but they failed completely. They could not harm them in any way whatever.

Motecuhzoma Learns of the Magicians' Failure

Therefore they hastened back to the city, to tell Motecuhzoma what the strangers were like and how invulnerable they were. They said to him: "Our lord, we are no match for them: we are mere nothings!" Motecuhzoma at once gave out orders: he commanded the officials and all the chiefs and captains, under the threat of death, to take the utmost pains to learn what the strangers needed and to provide it.

When the Spaniards left their ships and began to march here and were at last on the way, they were served and attended as they came and great honors were done them. They marched forward under protection, and everything possible was done to please them.

thirty-four

The Anxiety of Motecuhzoma and His People

Motecuhzoma was distraught and bewildered; he was filled with terror, not knowing what would happen to the city. The people were also terrified, debating the news among themselves. There were meetings and arguments and gossip in the street; there was weeping and lamenting. The people were downcast: they went about with their heads bowed down and greeted each other with tears.

But there were some who attempted to encourage their neighbors, and the children were caressed and comforted by their fathers and mothers. The chiefs said to Motecuhzoma, to fortify his heart: "The strangers are accompanied by a woman from this land, who speaks our Nahuatl tongue. She is called La Malinche, and she is from Teticpac. They found her there on the coast. . . ."

It was also at this time that the Spaniards asked so many questions about Motecuhzoma. They asked the villagers: "Is he a young man, or mature, or in his old age? Is he still vigorous, or does he feel himself to be growing old? Is he an old man now, with white hair?" The villagers replied: "He is a mature man, slender rather than stout, or even thin. Or not thin but lean, with a fine straight figure."

Motecuhzoma Thinks of Fleeing

When Motecuhzoma heard that they were inquiring about his person, and when he learned that the "gods" wished to see him face to face, his heart shrank within him and he was filled with anguish. He wanted to run away and hide; he thought of evading the "gods," of escaping to hide in a cave.

He spoke of this to certain trusted counselors who were not faint-hearted, whose hearts were still firm and resolute. They said: "There is the Place of the Dead, the House of the Sun, the Land of Tlaloc, or the Temple of Cintli.³ You should go to one or another, to whichever you prefer." Motecuhzoma knew what he desired: to go to the Temple of Cintli. And his desire was made known; it was revealed to the people.

But he could not do it. He could not run away, could not go into hiding. He had lost his strength and his spirit, and could do nothing. The magicians' words had overwhelmed his heart; they had vanquished his heart and thrown him into confusion, so that now he was weak and listless and too uncertain to make a decision.

Therefore he did nothing but wait. He did nothing but resign himself and wait for them to come. He mastered his heart at last, and waited for whatever was to happen.

[1] Small native fowl, which the Spaniards called "chickens of the land,"—that is, of Mexico. There were no true domesticated chickens in America until they were introduced from Europe.
[2] Who attended the Spaniards.
[3] Corn goddess.

Chapter Five

The Spaniards March on Tlaxcala and Cholula

Introduction

Despite the efforts of Motecuhzoma's envoys to keep the Spaniards from approaching Tenochtitlan, Cortes decided to march inland. The two indigenous accounts presented in this chapter— the first by Sahagun's informants, the second by the mestizo Munoz Camargo—describe the arrival of the Spaniards in Tlaxcala and Cholula. The account by the informants mentions the first battle between Spaniards and Indians (a group of Otomi Indians from Tecoac), after which the Tlaxcaltecas decided to receive the strangers in peace. As soon as the Spaniards arrived, the Tlaxcaltecas began to intrigue against nearby Cholula and the Aztecs.

There are two separate versions of what led the Spaniards to massacre the Indians in Cholula. According to Sahagun's informants, the massacre was inspired by the intrigues of the Tlaxcaltecas, whose "souls burned with hatred for the people of Cholula." According to Munoz Camargo, the Cholultecas brought their own destruction on themselves by not surrendering to Cortes and by treacherously murdering the envoy from Tlaxcala, Patlahuatzin, who advised them to form an alliance with the Spaniards. This second version may have been invented by the Tlaxcaltecas to excuse their part in the massacre; at least, there is no corroboration for it in either the *Historia* of Bernal Diaz del Castillo or the *Cartas de relacion* of Cortes.

The Spaniards March Inland

(From the *Codex Florentino* by Sahagun's informants)
At last they came. At last they began to march toward us.

A man from Cempoala, who was known as the Tlacochcalcatl [Chief of the House of Arrows], was the first official to welcome them as they entered our lands and cities. This man spoke Nahuatl. He showed them the best routes and the shortest ways; he guided and advised them, traveling at the head of the party.

When they came to Tecoac, in the land of the Tlaxcaltecas, they found it was inhabited by Otomies.[1] The Otomies came out to meet them in battle array; they greeted the strangers with their shields.

But the strangers conquered the Otomies of Tecoac; they utterly destroyed them. They divided their ranks, fired the cannons at them, attacked them with their swords and shot them with their crossbows. Not just a few, but all of them, perished in the battle.

And when Tecoac had been defeated, the Tlaxcaltecas

soon heard the news; they learned what had taken place there. They felt premonitions of death: terror overwhelmed them, and they were filled with foreboding.

Therefore the chiefs assembled; the captains met together in a council. They talked about what had happened, and said: "What shall we do? Shall we go out to meet them? The Otomi is a brave warrior, but he was helpless against them: they scorned him as a mere nothing! They destroyed the poor *macehual* with a look, with a glance of their eyes! We should go over to their side: we should make friends with them and be their allies. If not, they will destroy us too. . . ."

The Arrival at Tlaxcala

Therefore the lords of Tlaxcala went out to meet them, bringing many things to eat: hens and hens' eggs and the finest tortillas. They said to the strangers: "Our lords, you are weary."

The strangers replied: "Where do you live? Where are you from?"

They said: "We are from Tlaxcala. You have come here, you have entered our land. We are from Tlaxcala; our city is the City of the Eagle, Tlaxcala." (For in ancient times it was called Texcala, and its people were known as Texcaltecas.[2])

Then they guided them to the city; they brought them there and invited them to enter. They paid them great honors, attended to their every want, joined with them as allies and even gave them their daughters.

The Spaniards asked: "Where is the City of Mexico? Is it far from here?"

They said: "No, it is not far, it is only a three-day march. And it is a great city. The Aztecs are very brave. They are great warriors and conquerors and have defeated their neighbors on every side."

Intrigues Against Cholula

At this time the Tlaxcaltecas were enemies of Cholula. They feared the Cholultecas; they envied and cursed them; their souls burned with hatred for the people of Cholula. This is why they brought certain rumors to Cortes, so that he would destroy them. They said to him: "Cholula is our enemy. It is an evil city. The people are as brave as the Aztecs and they are the Aztecs' friends."

When the Spaniards heard this, they marched against Cholula. They were guided and accompanied by the Tlaxcaltecas and the chiefs from Cempoala, and they all marched in battle array.[3]

The Massacre at Cholula

When they arrived, the Tlaxcaltecas and the men of Cholula called to each other and shouted greetings. An assembly was held in the courtyard of the god, but when they had all gathered together, the entrances were closed, so that there was no way of escaping.

Then the sudden slaughter began: knife strokes, and sword strokes, and death. The people of Cholula had not foreseen it, had not suspected it. They faced the Spaniards without weapons, without their swords or their shields. The cause of the slaughter was treachery. They died blindly, without knowing why, because of the lies of the Tlaxcaltecas.

And when this had taken place, word of it was brought to Motecuhzoma. The messengers came and departed, journeying back and forth between Tenochtitlan and Cholula. The common people were terrified by the news; they could do nothing but tremble with fright. It was as if the earth trembled beneath them, or as if the world were spinning before their eyes, as it spins during a fit of vertigo. . . .

When the massacre at Cholula was complete, the strangers set out again toward the City of Mexico. They came in battle array, as conquerors, and the dust rose in whirlwinds on the roads. Their spears glinted in the sun, and their pennons fluttered like bats. They made a loud clamor as they marched, for their coats of mail and their weapons clashed and rattled. Some of them were dressed in glistening iron from head to foot; they terrified everyone who saw them.

Their dogs came with them, running ahead of the column. They raised their muzzles high; they lifted their muzzles to the wind. They raced on before with saliva dripping from their jaws.

Negotiations Before the Battle

(From the *Historia de Tlaxcala* by Diego Munoz Camargo)

From this time forward, the Spaniards had no other purpose than to raise soldiers against the Culhuas Mexicanos.[4] They

The Massacre at Cholula (Lienzo de Tlaxcala)

forty-two

did this within a very short time, so as to give them no opportunity to form an alliance with the Tlaxcaltecas. And to avoid bad thoughts, as well as other new incidents and proposals, Cortes saw to it that his new friends and confederates did not leave his side, using his wits as always, as an astute leader, to take advantage of a favorable situation.

When the ranks were formed, the Spanish troops and the Tlaxcaltecas marched out in good military order, with enough supplies for their great undertaking and with many important and famous captains, all skilled in warfare according to their ancient customs and practices. These captains were Piltecuhtli, Acxoxecatl, Tecpanecatl, Cahuecahua, Cocomitecuhtli, Quauhtotohua, Textlipitl and many others; but because they were so many, with such a variety of names, the others are not set down here, only the most outstanding, who were always loyal to Cortes until the end of his conquest.

The first invasion took place at Cholula, which was governed and ruled by two lords, Tlaquiach and Tlalchiac (for the lords who succeeded to that command were always known by those names, which mean "Lord of what is above" and "Lord of what is below").

Once they entered the province of Cholula, the Spaniards quickly destroyed that city because of the great provocations given by its inhabitants. So many Cholultecas were killed in this invasion that the news raced through the land as far as the City of Mexico. There it caused the most horrible fright and consternation, for it was also known that the Tlaxcaltecas had allied themselves with the "gods" (as the Spaniards were called in all parts of this New World, for want of another name).

The Cholultecas had placed such confidence in their idol Quetzalcoatl that they believed no human power could defeat or harm them. They thought they would be able to vanquish us in a very short time—first, because the Spaniards were so few, and second, because the Tlaxcaltecas had brought them against Cholula by deceit. Their faith in the idol was so complete that they believed it would ravage their enemies with the fire and thunder of heaven, and drown them in a vast flood of water.

This is what they believed, and they proclaimed it in loud voices: "Let the strangers come! We will see if they are so powerful! Our god Quetzalcoatl is here with us, and they can never defeat him. Let them come, the weaklings: we are waiting to see them, and we laugh at their stupid delusions. They are fools or madmen if they trust in these sodomites from Tlaxcala, who are nothing but their women. And let the hirelings come, too: they have sold themselves in their terror. Look at the scum of Tlaxcala, the cowards of Tlaxcala, the guilty ones! They were conquered by the City of Mexico, and now they bring strangers to defend them! How could you change so soon? How could you put yourselves into the hands of these foreign savages? Oh, you frightened beggars, you have lost the immortal glory that was won by your heroes, who sprang from the pure blood of the ancient Teochichimecas, the founders of your nation. What will become of you, you traitors? We are waiting, and you will see how our god Quetzalcoatl punishes his foes!"

They shouted these and other similar insults, because they believed that the enemy would surely be consumed by bolts of fire which would fall from heaven, and that great rivers of water would pour from the temples of their idols to drown both the Tlaxcaltecas and the Spanish soldiers. This caused the Tlaxcaltecas no little fear and concern, for they believed that all would happen as the Cholultecas predicted, and the priests of the temple of Quetzalcoatl proclaimed it at the top of their voices.

But when the Tlaxcaltecas heard the Spaniards call out to St. James, and saw them burn the temples and hurl the idols to the ground, profaning them with great zeal and determination, and when they also saw that the idols were powerless, that no flames fell and no rivers poured out—then they understood the deception and knew it was all falsehoods and lies.

Thus encouraged, they grew so brave that the slaughter and havoc increased beyond imagining. Our friends also became well aware of the Spaniards' courage; they never again plotted any crimes, but were guided by the divine order, which was to serve Our Lord by conquering this land and rescuing it from the power of the devil.

Before the battle began, the city of Tlaxcala sent messengers and ambassadors to Cholula to ask for peace and to say that they were marching not against the Cholultecas but against the Culhuas, or Culhuacanenses Mexicanos. (They were called Culhuas, it is said, because they had come from the region of Culhuacan in the West; and Mexicanos, because the city which they founded and made supreme was called Mexico.) The envoys told the Cholultecas that they were marching under the command of Cortes and that they came desiring peace. They said that the people of Cholula should fear no harm from the bearded strangers, for these were a very great and noble people who only sought their friendship. Thus they begged the Cholultecas as friends to receive the strangers in peace, because they would be well used by them and suffer no ill treatment, but they also warned them not to anger the white men, for they were a very warlike, daring and valiant people, who carried superior weapons made of white metal. They said this because there was no iron among the natives, only copper.

They also said that the strangers brought arms which could shoot fire, and wild animals on leashes; that they were dressed and shod in iron, and had powerful crossbows, and lions and ounces so ferocious that they ate people (meaning the fierce greyhounds and mastiffs which the Spaniards had brought with them); and that against this might the Cholultecas could not prevail, or even defend themselves, if they angered the "gods" and did not surrender peacefully, as they should do to avoid greater harm. And they counseled them as friends to act in this manner.

Death of the Envoy from Tlaxcala

But the Cholultecas paid no attention to these words, preferring to die rather than surrender. Rejecting the good counsel of the Tlaxcaltecas, they flayed the face of Patlahuatzin, the ambassador, a man of great repute and valor. They did the same to his arms, which they flayed to the elbows, and they cut his hands at the wrists so that they dangled. In this cruel fashion they sent him away, saying: "Go back, and tell the Tlaxcaltecas and those other beggars, or gods, or whatever they are, that this is how we invite them to come. This is the answer we send them."

The ambassador returned in great agony, victim of an outrage that caused much horror and grief in the republic, because he was one of the worthiest and most handsome men of this land. He died in the service of his homeland and republic, where his fame is eternal among his people, who keep his memory alive in their songs and sayings.

The Tlaxcaltecas were enraged at this inhuman treatment of Patlahuatzin. They took such unthinkable cruelty as a great affront, since all ambassadors were traditionally respected and honored by foreign kings and lords, to whom they reported the treaties, wars and other events that took place in these provinces and kingdoms. Therefore they said to Cortes: "Most valiant lord, we wish to accompany you, in order to seek vengeance against Cholula for its insolent wickedness, and to conquer and destroy that city and its province. A people so obstinate and vicious, so evil and tyrannous, should not remain alive. And if there were no other cause than this, they would deserve eternal punishment, for they have not thanked us for our good counsel, but have scorned and despised us because of our love for you."

The valiant Cortes answered them with a stern face: "Have no fear. I promise you revenge." And he kept this promise, waging a cruel war in which vast multitudes were slaughtered, as is recorded in the chronicles.

The Cholultecas said that their foes would all be drowned by their idol Quetzalcoatl. This was the most venerated idol among the many that were worshipped in this land, and its temple at Cholula was considered a shrine of the gods. They said that when the crust was scraped from a portion of the limed surface of the temple, water gushed out. To save themselves from drowning, they sacrificed children of two or three years of age and mixed their blood with lime to make a kind of cement with which to stop up the springs and founts. They said that if they were ever in danger during a war with the white gods and the Tlaxcaltecas, they would break open all the mortared surfaces, from which a flood of water would pour forth to drown their enemies. And when they saw how hard pressed they were, they set to work.

The Destruction of Cholula

But none of their expectations was fulfilled, and they lost all hope. Of those who died in the battle of Cholula, the greater number hurled themselves from the temple pyramid in their despair and they also hurled the idol of Quetzalcoatl headfirst from the pyramid, for this form of suicide had always been a custom among them. They were as rebellious and contemptuous as any stiff-necked, ungovernable people, and it was their custom to die in a manner contrary to that of other nations— that is, to die headlong. In the end, the greater part of them died in despair, by killing themselves.

When the battle of Cholula was finished, the Cholultecas understood and believed that the God of the white men, who were His most powerful sons, was more potent than their own. Our friends the Tlaxcaltecas, seeing themselves in the very thick of that battle and massacre, called upon St. James the Apostle, shouting his name in loud voices: "Santiago!" And from that day to this, when they are in some difficulty or danger, the Tlaxcaltecas invoke the saint.

They made use of a very good counsel given them by Cortes, so that they could be distinguished and would not die among the enemy by mistake. Since their weapons and emblems and those of the enemy were almost the same, with only the slightest differences, and since there was such a great multitude of people on both sides, some means of identification was a necessity. Otherwise, in the press of battle, they would have killed their own warriors without knowing it. Therefore they wore plaited garlands of feather-grass on their heads, in order to recognize each other; and the counsel proved to be of considerable value.

When Cholula had been stormed and destroyed, and a great host of people killed and plundered, our armies marched forward again, causing terror wherever they went, until the news of the destruction spread through the whole land. The people were astonished to hear such strange reports, and to learn how the Cholultecas were defeated and slain in so short a time, and how their idol Quetzalcoatl had not served them in any way.

[1] One of the tribes that had settled in the Valley of Mexico (and elsewhere) long before the arrival of the Aztecs.

[2] Texcala: "Where there are many rocks." The Aztecs explained the origin of the word Tlaxcala in this way, but to the Tlaxcaltecas it means "where there are corn tortillas."

[3] This was customary and therefore roused no suspicion among the Cholultecas.

[4] The Aztecs. (The term is explained later in the text.)

Chapter Six

The Gifts of Gold:
The God Tezcatlipoca Appears

Introduction

After the destruction of Cholula, the Spaniards continued to march toward the Valley of Mexico, accompanied by their allies from Tlaxcala. The texts by Sahagun's informants, from which the passages in this chapter are taken, describe two incidents of particular interest.

When the army was among the volcanoes, in what the Indians called the Eagle Pass, it was met by new envoys from Motecuhzoma, headed by Tzihuacpopocatzin. The envoys presented many objects of gold to the strangers, and then observed their reactions to the gifts: "The Spaniards burst into smiles. . . . They hungered like pigs for that gold. . . ."

Second, the texts report the deceit of Tzihuacpopocatzin, who attempted—apparently on Motecuhzoma's orders—to pass himself off as Motecuhzoma. This effort failed, and another series of envoys was sent out—magicians again—in the hope of stopping the conquistadors. But the wizards retired before the mysterious presence of a pretended drunkard, who foretold the ruin of Mexico and showed them portents. They thought the god Tezcatlipoca had appeared to them, and they hurried back to Tenochtitlan to tell Motecuhzoma. The great Aztec *tlatoani* was even more depressed than before and waited fatalistically for what was to come.

The Spaniards See the Objects of Gold

Then Motecuhzoma dispatched various chiefs. Tzihuac-popocatzin was at their head, and he took with him a great many of his representatives. They went out to meet the Spaniards in the vicinity of Popocatepetl and Iztactepetl, there in the Eagle Pass.

They gave the "gods" ensigns of gold, and ensigns of quetzal feathers, and golden necklaces. And when they were given these presents, the Spaniards burst into smiles; their eyes shone with pleasure; they were delighted by them. They picked up the gold and fingered it like monkeys; they seemed to be transported by joy, as if their hearts were illumined and made new.

The truth is that they longed and lusted for gold. Their bodies swelled with greed, and their hunger was ravenous; they hungered like pigs for that gold. They snatched at the golden ensigns, waved them from side to side and examined every inch of them. They were like one who speaks a barbarous tongue: everything they said was in a barbarous tongue.

Tzihuacpopocatzin Pretends to Be Motecuhzoma

When they saw Tzihuacpopocatzin, they asked: "Is this Motecuhzoma, by any chance?" They asked this of their allies, the liars from Tlaxcala and Cempoala, their shrewd and deceitful confederates.

They replied: "He is not Motecuhzoma, our lords. He is his envoy Tzihuacpopocatzin."

The Spaniards asked him: "Are you Motecuhzoma, by any chance?"

"Yes," he said, "I am your servant. I am Motecuhzoma."

But the allies said: "You fool! Why try to deceive us? Who do you think we are?" And they said:

"You cannot deceive us; you cannot make fools of us.
You cannot frighten us; you cannot blind our eyes.
You cannot stare us down; we will not look away.
You cannot bewitch our eyes or turn them aside.
You cannot dim our eyes or make them swoon.
You cannot fill them with dust or shut them with slime.

"You are not Motecuhzoma: he is there in his city.
He cannot hide from us. Where can he go?
Can he fly away like a bird? Can he tunnel the earth?
Can he burrow into a mountain, to hide inside it?
We are coming to see him, to meet him face to face.
We are coming to hear his words from his own lips."

They taunted and threatened the envoys in this fashion, and the gifts of welcome and the greetings were another failure. Therefore the envoys hastened back to the city.

The Apparition of Tezcatlipoca

But then there was another series of envoys: magicians, wizards and priests. They also left the city and went out to meet the strangers, but they were completely helpless: they could not blind their eyes or overcome them in any way.

They even failed to meet and speak with the "gods," because a certain drunkard blundered across their path. He used the gestures that are used by the people of Chalco, and he was dressed like a Chalca, with eight cords of couch-grass across his breast. He seemed to be very drunk; he feigned drunkenness; he pretended to be a drunkard.

He came up to them while they were about to meet the Spaniards. He rushed up to the Mexicanos and cried: "Why have you come here? For what purpose? What is it you want? What is Motecuhzoma trying to do? Has he still not recovered his wits? Does he still tremble and beg? He has committed many errors and destroyed a multitude of people. Some have been beaten and others wrapped in shrouds; some have been betrayed and others mocked and derided."

When the magicians heard these words, they tried in vain to approach him. They wanted to ask his help, and they hurriedly built him a small temple and altar and a seat made of couch-grass. But for a while they could not see him.

They labored in vain, they prepared his temple in vain, for he spoke to them only in oracles. He terrified them with his harsh reproofs and spoke to them as if from a great distance: "Why have you come here? It is useless. Mexico will be destroyed! Mexico will be left in ruins!" He said: "Go back, go back! Turn your eyes toward the city. What was fated to happen has already taken place!"

They looked in the direction of Tenochtitlan. The temples were in flames, and so were the communal halls, the religious schools and all the houses. It was as if a great battle were raging in the city.

When the magicians saw this, they lost heart. They could not speak clearly, but talked as if they were drunk: "It was not proper for us to have seen this vision. Motecuhzoma himself should have beheld it! This was not a mere mortal. This was the young Tezcatlipoca!"

Suddenly the god disappeared, and they saw him no longer. The envoys did not go forward to meet the Spaniards; they did not speak with them. The priests and magicians turned and went back to report to Motecuhzoma.

Motecuhzoma's Despair

When the envoys arrived in the city, they told Motecuhzoma what had happened and what they had seen. Motecuhzoma listened to their report and then bowed his head without speaking a word. For a long time he remained thus, with his head bent down. And when he spoke at last, it was only to say: "What help is there now, my friends? Is there a mountain for us to climb? Should we run away? We are Mexicanos: would this bring any glory to the Mexican nation?

"Pity the old men, and the old women, and the innocent

little children. How can they save themselves? But there is no help. What can we do? Is there nothing left us?

"We will be judged and punished. And however it may be, and whenever it may be, we can do nothing but wait."

Chapter Seven

The Spaniards Are Welcomed in Tezcoco

Introduction

The Spaniards pushed on toward Tenochtitlan, coming down out of the mountains by way of Tlalmanalco. Shortly after their descent, Prince Ixtlilxochitl of Tezcoco (brother of Cacama, the lord of Tezcoco) left his city with a group of followers to greet Cortes in peace.

The *Codex Ramirez* preserves a few fragments in Spanish of an older, indigenous account of this episode, of which the Nahuatl original has been lost. According to this account, it was Prince Ixtlilxochitl who persuaded the people of Tezcoco, resentful of Aztec domination, to join forces with the conquistadors. The same account states that Cortes then visited the city of Tezcoco, but this statement is not corroborated in any other source. Bernal Diaz del Castillo, Sahagun's informants and Fernando de Alva Ixtlilxochitl do not mention such a visit; they say only that the Spaniards marched to Ixtapalapa and from there to the Aztec capital. The *Codex Ramirez* contains several anecdotes of interest and importance, especially the reaction of Yacotzin, the prince's mother, when her son asked her to change her religion. It also describes how Motecuhzoma responded to the news that the Spaniards were approaching Tezcoco. He ordered a last meeting of his chiefs, to discuss whether the strangers should be welcomed or repulsed when they arrived at Tenochtitlan. Despite Cuitlahuac's gloomy predictions, he finally decided to receive them in peace.

The March to Tezcoco

When the Spaniards looked down from the mountain heights, they were delighted to see so many villages and towns. Some suggested that they should return to Tlaxcala until they could increase their forces, but Cortes urged them on, and the march to Tezcoco was begun.

They spent that night in the mountains and set out again the next day. After they had marched a few miles, they were met by Ixtlilxochitl and his brothers with a large company of followers. Cortes distrusted them at first; but when he learned, through signs and translations, that they had come out to meet the Spaniards as friends, he was greatly pleased. The Christians pointed to their Captain, and Ixtlilxochitl approached him and greeted him with smiles and obeisances, to which Cortes responded in the Spanish fashion. The prince was astonished to see a man with such white skin and with a beard and with so much courage and majesty, while Cortes, in turn, was astonished by the prince and his brothers—especially by Tecocoltzin, who was as white as any of the Spaniards.

At last, with La Malinche and Aguilar as interpreters, Ixtlilxochitl begged Cortes to accompany him to Tezcoco, so that he and his people might serve him. Cortes thanked the prince and accepted his invitation.

The Arrival at the City

At the request of Ixtlilxochitl, Cortes and his men ate the gifts of food that had been brought out from Tezcoco. Then they walked to the city with their new friends, and all the people came out to cheer and welcome them. The Indians knelt down and adored them as sons of the Sun, their gods, believing that the time had come of which their dear king Nezahualpilli[1] had so often spoken. The Spaniards entered the city and were lodged in the royal palace.

Word of these events was brought to the king, Motecuhzoma, who was pleased by the reception his nephews had given Cortes. He was also pleased by what Cohuamacotzin and Ixtlilxochitl had said to the Captain, because he believed that Ixtlilxochitl would call in the garrisons stationed on the frontiers. But God ordered it otherwise.

Cortes was very grateful for the attentions shown him by Ixtlilxochitl and his brothers; he wished to repay their kindness by teaching them the law of God, with the help of his interpreter Aguilar. The brothers and a number of the other lords gathered to hear him, and he told them that the emperor of the Christians had sent him here, so far away, in order that he might instruct them in the law of Christ. He explained the mystery of the Creation and the Fall, the mystery of the Trinity and the Incarnation and the mystery of the Passion and the Resurrection. Then he drew out a crucifix and held it up. The Christians all knelt, and Ixtlilxochitl and the other lords knelt with them.

Cortes also explained the mystery of Baptism. He concluded the lesson by telling them how the Emperor Charles grieved that they were not in God's grace, and how the emperor had sent him among them only to save their souls. He begged them to become willing vassals of the emperor, because that was the will of the pope, in whose name he spoke.

Ixtlilxochitl Becomes a Christian

When Cortes asked for their reply, Ixtlilxochitl burst into tears and answered that he and his brothers understood the mysteries very well. Giving thanks to God that his soul had been illumined, he said that he wished to become a Christian and to serve the emperor. He begged for the crucifix, so that he and his brothers might worship it, and the Spaniards wept with joy to see their devotion.

The princes then asked to be baptized. Cortes and the priest accompanying him said that first they must learn more of the Christian religion, but that persons would be sent to instruct them. Ixtlilxochitl expressed his gratitude, but begged to receive the sacrament at once because he now hated all idolatry and revered the mysteries of the true faith.

Although a few of the Spaniards objected, Cortes decided that Ixtlilxochitl should be baptized immediately. Cortes himself served as godfather, and the prince was given the name Hernando, because that was his sponsor's name. His brother Cohuamacotzin was named Pedro because his godfather was Pedro de Alvarado, and Tecocoltzin was named Fernando, with Cortes sponsoring him also. The other Christians became godfathers to the other princes, and the baptisms were performed with the greatest solemnity. If it had been possible, more than twenty thousand persons would have been baptized that very day, and a great number of them did receive the sacrament.

The Reactions of Yacotzin

Ixtlilxochitl went to his mother, Yacotzin, to tell her what had happened and to bring her out to be baptized. She replied that he must have lost his mind to let himself be won over so easily by that handful of barbarians, the conquistadors. Don Hernando said that if she were not his mother, he would answer her by cutting off her head. He told her that she would receive the sacrament, even against her will, because nothing was important except the life of the soul.

Yacotzin asked her son to leave her alone for the time being. She said she would think about what he had told her and make her decision the next day. He left the palace and ordered her rooms to be set on fire (though others say that he found her in a temple of idolatry).

Finally she came out, saying that she wanted to become a a Christian. She went to Cortes and was baptized with a great many others. Cortes himself was her godfather, naming her Dona Maria because she was the first woman in Tezcoco to become a Christian. Her four daughters, the princesses, were also baptized, along with many other women. And during the three or four days they were in the city, the Spaniards baptized a great multitude of people.

Motecuhzoma's Final Decision

When Motecuhzoma learned what had happened in Tezcoco, he called together his nephew Cacama, his brother Cuitlahuac and the other lords. He proposed a long discussion in order to decide whether they should welcome the Christians when they arrived, and if so, in what manner. Cuitlahuac replied that they should not welcome them in any manner, but Cacama disagreed, saying that it would show a want of courage to deny them entrance once they were at the gates. He added that it was not proper for a great lord like his uncle to turn away the ambassadors of another great prince. If the visitors made any demands which displeased Motecuhzoma, he could punish their insolence by sending his hosts of brave warriors against them.

Before any one else could speak, Motecuhzoma announced that he agreed with his nephew. Cuitlahuac warned him: "I pray to our gods that you will not let the strangers into your house. They will cast you out of it and overthrow your rule, and when you try to recover what you have lost, it will be too late." With this the council came to an end. The other lords all showed by their gestures that they approved of this last opinion, but Motecuhzoma was resolved to welcome the Christians as friends. He told his nephew Cacama to go out to meet them and sent his brother Cuitlahuac to wait for them in the palace at Ixtapalapa.

[1] See Chapter 2, note 4.

Chapter Eight

The Spaniards Arrive in Tenochtitlan

Introduction

The Spaniards continued their march toward the Aztec capital, accompanied by all the allies they had brought with them from the Tlaxcala region. The account given in the texts by Sahagun's informants, from which the passages in this chapter are drawn, begins with a description of the order in which the various sections of the army made their appearance. They approached the island city from the south, by way of Ixtapalapa, and arrived in Xoloco (later called San Anton and now part of the Avenue of San Antonio Abad) on November 8, 1519. The precise date is recorded in the *XIII relacion* of Fernando de Alva Ixtilxochitl.

When Cortes and Motecuhzoma finally met at Huitzillan, on the same avenue, they greeted each other in speeches that have been carefully preserved by Sahagun's informants. The texts then describe the stay of the conquistadors in Tenochtitlan and their greed for the gold objects stored in the treasure houses.

Motecuhzoma Goes Out to Meet Cortes

The Spaniards arrived in Xoloco, near the entrance to Tenochtitlan. That was the end of the march, for they had reached their goal.

Motecuhzoma now arrayed himself in his finery, preparing to go out to meet them. The other great princes also adorned their persons, as did the nobles and their chieftains and knights. They all went out together to meet the strangers.

They brought trays heaped with the finest flowers—the flower that resembles a shield; the flower shaped like a heart; in the center, the flower with the sweetest aroma; and the fragrant yellow flower, the most precious of all. They also brought garlands of flowers, and ornaments for the breast, and necklaces of gold, necklaces hung with rich stones, necklaces fashioned in the petatillo style.

Thus Motecuhzoma went out to meet them, there in Huitzillan. He presented many gifts to the Captain and his commanders, those who had come to make war. He showered gifts upon them and hung flowers around their necks; he gave them necklaces of flowers and bands of flowers to adorn their breasts; he set garlands of flowers upon their heads. Then he hung the gold necklaces around their necks and gave them presents of every sort as gifts of welcome.

Speeches of Motecuhzoma and Cortes

When Motecuhzoma had given necklaces to each one, Cortes asked him: "Are you Motecuhzoma? Are you the king? Is it true that you are the king Motecuhzoma?"

And the king said: "Yes, I am Motecuhzoma." Then he stood up to welcome Cortes; he came forward, bowed his head low and addressed him in these words: "Our lord, you are weary. The journey has tired you, but now you have arrived on the earth. You have come to your city, Mexico. You have come here to sit on your throne, to sit under its canopy.

"The kings who have gone before, your representatives, guarded it and preserved it for your coming. The kings Itzcoatl, Motecuhzoma the Elder, Axayacatl, Tizoc and Ahuitzol ruled for you in the City of Mexico. The people were protected by their swords and sheltered by their shields.

"Do the kings know the destiny of those they left behind, their posterity? If only they are watching! If only they can see what I see!

"No, it is not a dream. I am not walking in my sleep. I am not seeing you in my dreams. . . . I have seen you at last! I have met you face to face! I was in agony for five days, for ten days, with my eyes fixed on the Region of the Mystery. And now you have come out of the clouds and mists to sit on your throne again.

"This was foretold by the kings who governed your city, and now it has taken place. You have come back to us; you have come down from the sky. Rest now, and take possession of your royal houses. Welcome to your land, my lords!"

When Motecuhzoma had finished, La Malinche translated his address into Spanish so that the Captain could understand it. Cortes replied in his strange and savage tongue, speaking first to La Malinche: "Tell Motecuhzoma that we are his friends. There is nothing to fear. We have wanted to see him for a long time, and now we have seen his face and heard his words. Tell him that we love him well and that our hearts are contented." Then he said to Motecuhzoma: "We have come to your house in Mexico as friends. There is nothing to fear."

La Malinche translated this speech and the Spaniards grasped Motecuhzoma's hands and patted his back to show their affection for him.

Attitudes of the Spaniards and the Native Lords

The Spaniards examined everything they saw. They dismounted from their horses, and mounted them again, and dismounted again, so as not to miss anything of interest.

The chiefs who accompanied Motecuhzoma were: Cacama, king of Tezcoco; Tetlepanquetzaltzin, king of Tlacopan; Itzcuauhtzin the Tlacochcalcatl, lord of Tlatelolco; and Topantemoc, Motecuhzoma's treasurer in Tlatelolco. These four chiefs were standing in a file.

The other princes were: Atlixcatzin [chief who has taken captives][1]; Tepeoatzin, The Tlacochcalcatl; Quetzalaztatzin, the keeper of the chalk; Totomotzin; Hecateupatiltzin; and Cuappiatzin.

When Motecuhzoma was imprisoned, they all went into hiding. They ran away to hide and treacherously abandoned him!

The Spaniards Take Possession of the City

When the Spaniards entered the Royal House, they placed Motecuhzoma under guard and kept him under their vigilance. They also placed a guard over Itzcuauhtzin, but the other lords were permitted to depart.

Then the Spaniards fired one of their cannons, and this caused great confusion in the city. The people scattered in every direction; they fled without rhyme or reason; they ran off as if they were being pursued. It was as if they had eaten the mushrooms that confuse the mind, or had seen some dreadful apparition. They were all overcome by terror, as if their hearts had fainted. And when night fell, the panic spread through the city and their fears would not let them sleep.

In the morning the Spaniards told Motecuhzoma what they needed in the way of supplies: tortillas, fried chickens, hens' eggs, pure water, firewood and charcoal. Also: large, clean cooking pots, water jars, pitchers, dishes and other pottery. Motecuhzoma ordered that it be sent to them. The chiefs who received this order were angry with the king and no longer revered or respected him. But they furnished the Spaniards with all the provisions they needed—food, beverages and water, and fodder for the horses.

The Spaniards Reveal Their Greed

When the Spaniards were installed in the palace, they asked Motecuhzoma about the city's resources and reserves and about the warriors' ensigns and shields. They questioned him closely and then demanded gold.

Motecuhzoma guided them to it. They surrounded him and crowded close with their weapons. He walked in the center, while they formed a circle around him.

When they arrived at the treasure house called Teucalco,

The Spaniards Melting Gold Objects (Codex Florentino)

sixty-seven

the riches of gold and feathers were brought out to them: ornaments made of quetzal feathers, richly worked shields, disks of gold, the necklaces of the idols, gold nose plugs, gold greaves and bracelets and crowns.

The Spaniards immediately stripped the feathers from the gold shields and ensigns. They gathered all the gold into a great mound and set fire to everything else, regardless of its value. Then they melted down the gold into ingots. As for the precious green stones, they took only the best of them; the rest were snatched up by the Tlaxcaltecas. The Spaniards searched through the whole treasure house, questioning and quarreling, and seized every object they thought was beautiful.

The Seizure of Motecuhzoma's Treasures

Next they went to Motecuhzoma's storehouse, in the place called Totocalco [Place of the Palace of the Birds],[2] where his personal treasures were kept. The Spaniards grinned like little beasts and patted each other with delight.

When they entered the hall of treasures, it was as if they had arrived in Paradise. They searched everywhere and coveted everything; they were slaves to their own greed. All of Motecuhzoma's possessions were brought out: fine bracelets, necklaces with large stones, ankle rings with little gold bells, the royal crowns and all the royal finery—everything that belonged to the king and was reserved to him only. They seized these treasures as if they were their own, as if this plunder were merely a stroke of good luck. And when they had taken all the gold, they heaped up everything else in the middle of the patio.

La Malinche called the nobles together. She climbed up to the palace roof and cried: "Mexicanos, come forward! The Spaniards need your help! Bring them food and pure water. They are tired and hungry; they are almost fainting from exhaustion! Why do you not come forward? Are you angry with them?"

The Mexicans were too frightened to approach. They were crushed by terror and would not risk coming forward. They shied away as if the Spaniards were wild beasts, as if the hour were midnight on the blackest night of the year. Yet they did not abandon the Spaniards to hunger and thirst. They brought them whatever they needed, but shook with fear as they did so. They delivered the supplies to the Spaniards with trembling hands, then turned and hurried away.

[1] Military title given to a warrior who had captured four enemies.
[2] The zoological garden attached to the royal palaces.

Chapter Nine

The Massacre in the Main Temple During the Fiesta of Toxcatl

Introduction

Several indigenous texts—the *Codex Ramirez*, the *XIII relacion* of Alva Ixtlilxochitl and the *Codex Aubin*—describe the massacre perpetrated during the fiesta of Toxcatl, which the Aztecs celebrated in honor of the god Huitzilopochtli. "This was the most important of their fiestas," wrote Sahagun. "It was like our Easter and fell at almost the same time."

Cortes had been absent from the city for twenty days when the massacre took place; he had gone out to fight Panfilo de Narvaez, who was coming to arrest him by order of Diego Velazques, governor of Cuba. Cortes' deputy, Pedro de Alvarado, treacherously murdered the celebrants when the festival was at its height.

We have chosen two different accounts of the massacre, both written originally in Nahuatl. They describe it with a realism comparable to that of the great epic poems of classical antiquity.

The first account, by Sahagun's native informants, tells of the preparations for the fiesta, the sudden attack by the Spaniards in the midst of the ceremonies and the retaliation by the Indians, who besieged the Spaniards when they took refuge in Motecuhzoma's palace.

The second brief account is by the native author of the *Codex Aubin*. "From a literary standpoint," says Dr. Garibay, "the passage is of extraordinary merit. It shows us the living, suffering people of Tenochtitlan as they faced the attack of the Tonatiuh (Alvarado), who was as handsome as he was wicked."

The Preparations for the Fiesta

The Aztecs begged permission of their king to hold the fiesta of Huitzilopochtli. The Spaniards wanted to see this fiesta to learn how it was celebrated. A delegation of the celebrants came to the palace where Motecuhzoma was a prisoner, and when their spokesman asked his permission, he granted it to them.

As soon as the delegation returned, the women began to grind seeds of the chicalote.[1] These women had fasted for a whole year. They ground the seeds in the patio of the temple.

The Spaniards came out of the palace together, dressed in armor and carrying their weapons with them. They stalked among the women and looked at them one by one; they stared into the faces of the women who were grinding seeds. After this cold inspection, they went back into the palace. It is said that they planned to kill the celebrants if the men entered the patio.

The Statue of Huitzilopochtli

On the evening before the fiesta of Toxcatl, the celebrants began to model a statue of Huitzilopochtli. They gave it such a human appearance that it seemed the body of a living man. Yet they made the statue with nothing but a paste made of the ground seeds of the chicalote, which they shaped over an armature of sticks.

When the statue was finished, they dressed it in rich feathers, and they painted crossbars over and under its eyes. They also clipped on its earrings of turquoise mosaic; these were in the shape of serpents, with gold rings hanging from them. Its nose plug, in the shape of an arrow, was made of gold and was inlaid with fine stones.

They placed the magic headdress of hummingbird feathers on its head. They also adorned it with an *anecuyotl*, which was a belt made of feathers, with a cone at the back. Then they hung around its neck an ornament of yellow parrot feathers, fringed like the locks of a young boy. Over this they put its nettle-leaf cape, which was painted black and decorated with five clusters of eagle feathers.

Next they wrapped it in its cloak, which was painted with skulls and bones, and over this they fastened its vest. The vest was painted with dismembered human parts: skulls, ears, hearts, intestines, torsos, breasts, hands and feet. They also put on its *maxtlatl*, or loincloth,[2] which was decorated with images of dissevered limbs and fringed with amate paper.[3] This *maxtlatl* was painted with vertical stripes of bright blue.

They fastened a red paper flag at its shoulder and placed on its head what looked like a sacrificial flint knife. This too was made of red paper; it seemed to have been steeped in blood.

The statue carried a *tehuehuelli*, a bamboo shield decorated with four clusters of fine eagle feathers. The pendant of this shield was blood-red, like the knife and the shoulder flag. The statue also carried four arrows.

Finally, they put the wristbands on its arms. These bands, made of coyote skin, were fringed with paper cut into little strips.

The Beginning of the Fiesta

Early the next morning, the statue's face was uncovered by those who had been chosen for that ceremony. They gathered in front of the idol in single file and offered it gifts of food, such as round seedcakes or perhaps human flesh. But they did not carry it up to its temple on top of the pyramid.

All the young warriors were eager for the fiesta to begin. They had sworn to dance and sing with all their hearts, so that the Spaniards would marvel at the beauty of the rituals.

The procession began, and the celebrants filed into the temple patio to dance the Dance of the Serpent. When they were all together in the patio, the songs and the dance began. Those who had fasted for twenty days and those who had fasted for a year were in command of the others; they kept the dancers in file with their pine wands. (If anyone wished to urinate, he did not stop dancing, but simply opened his clothing at the hips and separated his clusters of heron feathers.)

If anyone disobeyed the leaders or was not in his proper place they struck him on the hips and shoulders. Then they drove him out of the patio, beating him and shoving him from behind. They pushed him so hard that he sprawled to the ground, and they dragged him outside by the ears. No one dared to say a word about this punishment, for those who had fasted during the year were feared and venerated; they had earned the exclusive title "Brothers of Huitzilopochtli."

The great captains, the bravest warriors, danced at the head of the files to guide the others. The youths followed at a slight distance. Some of the youths wore their hair gathered into large locks, a sign that they had never taken any captives. Others carried their headdresses on their shoulders; they had taken captives, but only with help.

Then came the recruits, who were called "the young warriors." They had each captured an enemy or two. The others called to them: "Come, comrades, show us how brave you are! Dance with all your hearts!"

The Spaniards Attack the Celebrants

At this moment in the fiesta, when the dance was loveliest and when song was linked to song, the Spaniards were siezed with an urge to kill the celebrants. They all ran forward, armed as if for battle. They closed the entrances and passageways, all the gates of the patio: the Eagle Gate in the lesser palace, the Gate of the Canestalk and the Gate of the Serpent of Mirrors. They posted guards so that no one could escape, and then rushed into the Sacred Patio to slaughter the celebrants. They came on foot, carrying their swords and their wooden or metal shields.

They ran in among the dancers, forcing their way to the

The Massacre in the Main Temple (Codex Duran)

seventy-five

place where the drums were played. They attacked the man who was drumming and cut off his arms. Then they cut off his head, and it rolled across the floor.

They attacked all the celebrants, stabbing them, spearing them, striking them with their swords. They attacked some of them from behind, and these fell instantly to the ground with their entrails hanging out. Others they beheaded: they cut off their heads, or split their heads to pieces.

They struck others in the shoulders, and their arms were torn from their bodies. They wounded some in the thigh and some in the calf. They slashed others in the abdomen, and their entrails all spilled to the ground. Some attempted to run away, but their intestines dragged as they ran; they seemed to tangle their feet in their own entrails. No matter how they tried to save themselves, they could find no escape.

Some attempted to force their way out, but the Spaniards murdered them at the gates. Others climbed the walls, but they could not save themselves. Those who ran into the communal houses were safe there for a while; so were those who lay down among the victims and pretended to be dead. But if they stood up again, the Spaniards saw them and killed them.

The blood of the warriors flowed like water and gathered into pools. The pools widened, and the stench of blood and entrails filled the air. The Spaniards ran into the communal houses to kill those who were hiding. They ran everywhere and searched everywhere; they invaded every room, hunting and killing.

The Aztecs Retaliate

When the news of this massacre was heard outside the Sacred Patio, a great cry went up: "Mexicanos, come running!

Bring your spears and shields! The strangers have murdered our warriors!"

This cry was answered with a roar of grief and anger: the people shouted and wailed and beat their palms against their mouths. The captains assembled at once, as if the hour had been determined in advance. They all carried their spears and shields.

Then the battle began. The Aztecs attacked with javelins and arrows, even with the light spears that are used for hunting birds. They hurled their javelins with all their strength, and the cloud of missiles spread out over the Spaniards like a yellow cloak.

The Spaniards immediately took refuge in the palace. They began to shoot at the Mexicans with their iron arrows and to fire their cannons and arquebuses. And they shackled Motecuhzoma in chains.

The Lament for the Dead

The Mexicans who had died in the massacre were taken out of the patio one by one and inquiries were made to discover their names. The fathers and mothers of the dead wept and lamented.

Each victim was taken first to his own home and then to the Sacred Patio, where all the dead were brought together. Some of the bodies were later burned in the place called the Eagle Urn, and others in the House of the Young Men.

Motecuhzoma's Message

At sunset, Itzcuauhtzin climbed onto the roof of the palace and shouted this proclamation: "Mexicanos! Tlatelolcas!

Your king, the lord Motecuhzoma, has sent me to speak for him. Mexicanos, hear me, for these are his words to you: 'We must not fight them. We are not their equals in battle. Put down your shields and arrows.'

"He tells you this because it is the aged who will suffer most, and they deserve your pity. The humblest classes will also suffer, and so will the innocent children who still crawl on all fours, who still sleep in their cradles.

"Therefore your king says: 'We are not strong enough to defeat them. Stop fighting, and return to your homes.' Mexicanos, they have put your king in chains; his feet are bound with chains."

When Itzcuauhtzin had finished speaking, there was a great uproar among the people. They shouted insults at him in their fury, and cried: "Who is Motecuhzoma to give us orders? We are no longer his slaves!" They shouted war cries and fired arrows at the rooftop. The Spaniards quickly hid Motecuhzoma and Itzcuauhtzin behind their shields so that the arrows would not find them.

The Mexicans were enraged because the attack on the captains had been so treacherous: their warriors had been killed without the slightest warning. Now they refused to go away or to put down their arms.

The Spaniards Are Besieged

The royal palace was placed under siege. The Mexicans kept a close watch to prevent anyone from stealing in with food for the Spaniards. They also stopped delivering supplies: they brought them absolutely nothing, and waited for them to die of hunger.

A few people attempted to communicate with the Spaniards. They hoped to win their favor by giving them advice and information or by secretly bringing them food. But the guards found them and killed them on the spot: they broke their necks or stoned them to death.

Once a group of porters was discovered bringing rabbit skins[4] into the city. They let slip the fact that other persons had been hiding in their midst. Therefore strict orders were issued to maintain a watch over all the roads and causeways leading to the city. The porters themselves had been sent by the chiefs of Ayotzintepec and Chinantlan. They were only performing their duties, but the guards seized them and put them to death for no reason. They would shout: "Here is another one!" and then kill him. And if they happened to see one of Motecuhzoma's servants with his glass lip plug, they slaughtered him at once, claiming: "He was bringing food to Motecuhzoma."

They seized anyone who was dressed like a porter or any other servant. "Here is another traitor," they would say. "He is bringing news to Motecuhzoma." The prisoner would try to save his life by pleading with them: "What are you doing, Mexicanos? I am not a traitor!" But they would answer: "Yes, you are. We know you are one of his servants." And they would immediately put him to death.

They stopped and examined everyone in the same way, studying each man's face and questioning him about his work. No one could walk out of doors without being arrested and accused. They sentenced a great many people for imaginary crimes; the victims were executed for acts they had never committed. The other servants, therefore, went home and hid themselves. They were afraid to be seen in public: they knew what would happen to them if they fell into the hands of the guards or the other warriors.

seventy-nine

After they had trapped the Spaniards in the palace, the Mexicans kept them under attack for seven days, and for twenty-three days they foiled all their attempts to break out. During this time all the causeways were closed off. The Mexicans tore up the bridges, opened great gaps in the pavement and built a whole series of barricades; they did everything they could to make the causeways impassable. They also closed off the roads by building walls and roadblocks; they obstructed all the roads and streets of the city.

The Massacre According to the Codex Aubin

Motecuhzoma said to La Malinche: "Please ask the god to hear me. It is almost time to celebrate the fiesta of Toxcatl. It will last for only ten days, and we beg his permission to hold it. We merely burn some incense and dance our dances. There will be a little noise because of the music, but that is all."

The Captain said: "Very well, tell him they may hold it." Then he left the city to meet another force of Spaniards who were marching in this direction. Pedro de Alvarado, called The Sun, was in command during his absence.

When the day of the fiesta arrived, Motecuhzoma said to The Sun: "Please hear me, my lord. We beg your permission to begin the fiesta of our god."

The Sun replied: "Let it begin. We shall be here to watch it."

The Aztec captains then called for their elder brothers, who were given this order: "You must celebrate the fiesta as grandly as possible."

The elder brothers replied: "We will dance with all our might."

Then Tecatzin, the chief of the armory, said: "Please remind the lord that he is here, not in Cholula. You know how they trapped the Cholultecas in their patio! They have already caused us enough trouble. We should hide our weapons close at hand!"

But Motecuhzoma said: "Are we at war with them? I tell you, we can trust them."

Tecatzin said: "Very well."

Then the songs and dances began. A young captain wearing a lip plug guided the dancers; he was Cuatlazol, from Tolnahuac.

But the songs had hardly begun when the Christians came out of the palace. They entered the patio and stationed four guards at each entrance. Then they attacked the captain who was guiding the dance. One of the Spaniards struck the idol in the face, and others attacked the three men who were playing the drums. After that there was a general slaughter until the patio was heaped with corpses.

A priest from the Place of the Canefields[5] cried out in a loud voice: "Mexicanos! Who said we are not at war? Who said we could trust them?"

The Mexicans could only fight back with sticks of wood; they were cut to pieces by the swords. Finally the Spaniards retired to the palace where they were lodged.

---

[1] *Argemone mexicana*, an edible plant, also used in medicines.

[2] Jacques Soustelle, in *La Vie quotidienne des Aztèques* (Paris: Hachette, 1955), describes the maxtlatl as "a cloth that was wrapped around the waist, passed between the legs and then tied in front, with the two ends hanging down in front and in back. These ends often had decorative borders or fringes. The maxtlatl was known to the Olmecs and Mayas during the earliest period of which we have any record. At the time of the Conquest, it was worn by all the civilized peoples of Mexico except the Tarascos in the West and the Huastecas in the Northeast, who were considered rather scandalous by the inhabitants of the central valley."

[3] A paper made from the inner bark of several different trees of the genus *Ficus*.

[4] The Aztecs had no cows, horses, pigs or other large domesticated animals. For leather and skins, therefore, they used the hides of deer and of such smaller creatures as the rabbit.

[5] A part of the main temple.

Chapter Ten

The Night of Sorrows

Introduction

After disposing of Panfilo de Narvaez, Cortes returned to the city, his ranks increased by troops from the defeated army. According to Sahagun's informants (from whose writings this chapter is drawn), the Aztecs planned to fall on him from ambush; but he reached the garrison in Tenochtitlan without hindrance and immediately ordered the cannons to be fired. The Aztecs responded by renewing their attack on the palace. The battle raged for four days. During a lull in the fighting, the Spaniards dragged the dead bodies of Motecuhzoma and Itzcuauhtzin to the water's edge. No one knows for certain how Motecuhzoma died.

It soon became obvious to Cortes that he would have to

abandon Tenochtitlan. He withdrew at night, but the retreat was discovered, and the Aztecs avenged themselves for the massacre in the temple patio. They attacked as the Spaniards were fleeing down the Tlacopan (now Tacuba) causeway, and the rout was so disastrous that it has been known ever since as "la noche triste," the Night of Sorrows. Those who escaped the disaster found refuge in the nearby village of Teocalhueyacan, where they were welcomed as friends; but three-fourths of the army had perished in the retreat and in the siege that preceded it.

The chapter concludes with a brief selection from the the *XIII relacion* by Alva Ixtilxochitl.

The Spaniards Abandon the City

At midnight the Spaniards and Tlaxcaltecas came out in closed ranks, the Spaniards going first and the Tlaxcaltecas following. The allies kept very close behind, as if they were crowding up against a wall. The sky was overcast and rain fell all night in the darkness, but it was a gentle rain, more like a drizzle or a heavy dew.

The Spaniards carried portable wooden bridges to cross the canals.[1] They set them in place, crossed over and raised them again. They were able to pass the first three canals—the Tecpantzinco, the Tzapotlan and the Atenchicalco—without being seen. But when they reached the fourth, the Mixcoatechi-altitlan, their retreat was discovered.

The Battle Begins

The first alarm was raised by a woman who was drawing water at the edge of the canal. She cried: "Mexicanos, come running! They are crossing the canal! Our enemies are escaping!"

Then a priest of Huitzilopochtli shouted the call to arms from the temple pyramid. His voice rang out over the city: "Captains, warriors, Mexicanos! Our enemies are escaping! Follow them in your boats.[2] Cut them off, and destroy them!"

When they heard this cry, the warriors leaped into the boats and set out in pursuit. These boats were from the garrisons of Tenochtitlan and Tlatelolco,[3] and were protected by the warriors' shields. The boatmen paddled with all their might; they lashed the water of the lake until it boiled.

Other warriors set out on foot, racing to Nonohualco and then to Tlacopan to cut off the retreat.

The boats converged on the Spaniards from both sides of the causeway, and the warriors loosed a storm of arrows at the fleeing army. But the Spaniards also turned to shoot at the Aztecs; they fired their crossbows and their arquebuses. The Spaniards and Tlaxcaltecas suffered many casualties, but many of the Aztec warriors were also killed or wounded.

The Massacre at the Canal of the Toltecs

When the Spaniards reached the Canal of the Toltecs, in Tlaltecayohuacan, they hurled themselves headlong into the water, as if they were leaping from a cliff.[4] The Tlaxcaltecas, the allies from Tliliuhquitepec, the Spanish foot soldiers and horsemen, the few women who accompanied the army—all came to the brink and plunged over it.

The canal was soon choked with the bodies of men and horses; they filled the gap in the causeway with their own

*The Spaniards and Their Allies Flee Down the Tlacopan
(Tacuba) Causeway* (Codex Florentino)

eighty-six

drowned bodies. Those who followed crossed to the other side by walking on the corpses.

When they reached Petlalco, where there was another canal, they crossed over on their portable bridge without being attacked by the Aztecs.[5] They stopped and rested there for a short while, and began to feel more like men again. Then they marched on to Popotla.

Dawn was breaking as they entered the village. Their hearts were cheered by the brightening light of this new day: they thought the horrors of the retreat by night were all behind them. But suddenly they heard war cries and the Aztecs swarmed through the streets and surrounded them. They had come to capture Tlaxcaltecas for their sacrifices. They also wanted to complete their revenge against the Spaniards.

The Aztecs harried the army all the way to Tlacopan. Chimalpopoca, the son of Motecuhzoma, was killed in the action at Tlilyuhcan by an arrow from the crossbows. Tlaltecat-zin, the Tepanec[6] prince, was wounded in the same action and died shortly after. He had served the Spaniards as a guide and advisor, pointing out the best roads and short cuts.

The Spaniards Take Refuge in Teocalhueyacan

Then the Spaniards forded a small river called the Tep-zolatl. Next they crossed two rivers, the Tepzolac and the Acueco, and stopped in Otoncalpulco, where the temple patio was surrounded by a wooden wall. They rested there in safety, catching their breath and recovering their strength.

While they were resting, the lord of Teocalhueyacan paid them a visit. He was known as The Otomi, a title reserved for the nobility. He greeted them and offered them the gifts of food his servants had brought: tortillas, eggs, roast chickens, a few live hens and various kinds of fruit. He placed these offerings in front of the Captain and said: "My lords, you are weary. You have suffered many heartaches. We beg the gods to rest now and enjoy these gifts."

La Malinche said: "My lord, the Captain wishes to know where you are from."

He answered: "Tell our lord that we are from Teocalhueyacan. Tell him that we hope he will visit us."

La Malinche said: "The Captain thanks you. We shall arrive tomorrow or the day after."

The Aztecs Recover the Spoils

As soon as it was daylight, the Aztecs cleared the dead Spaniards and Tlaxcaltecas out of the canals and stripped them of everything they wore. They loaded the bodies of the Tlaxcaltecas into canoes and took them out to where the rushes grow; they threw them among the rushes without burying them, without giving them another glance.

They also threw out the corpses of the women who had been killed in the retreat. The naked bodies of these women were the color of ripe corn, for they had painted themselves with yellow paint.

But they laid out the corpses of the Spaniards apart from the others; they lined them up in rows in a separate place. Their bodies were as white as the new buds of the canestalk, as white as the buds of the maguey. They also removed the dead "stags" that had carried the "gods" on their shoulders.

Then they gathered up everything the Spaniards had abandoned in their terror. When a man saw something he wanted, he took it, and it became his property; he hefted it onto his shoulders and carried it home. They also collected all the weapons that had been left behind or had fallen into the canal—the cannons, arquebuses, swords, spears, bows and arrows—along with all the steel helmets, coats of mail and breastplates, and the shields of metal, wood and hide. They recovered the gold ingots, the gold disks, the tubes of gold dust and the *chalchihuite* collars with their gold pendants.

They gathered up everything they could find and searched the waters of the canal with the greatest care. Some of them groped with their hands and others felt about with their feet. Those who went first were able to keep their balance but those who came along behind them all fell into the water.

The Account by Alva Ixtlilxochitl

Cortes turned in the direction of Tenochtitlan and entered the city of Tezcoco. He was received only by a group of knights, because the legitimate sons of King Nezahualpilli had been hidden by their servants, and the other lords were being held by the Aztecs as hostages. He entered Tenochtitlan with his army of Spaniards and allies on the day of St. John the Baptist, without being molested in any way.

The Mexicans gave them everything they needed, but when they saw that Cortes had no intention of leaving the city or of freeing their leaders, they rallied their warriors and attacked the Spaniards. This attack began on the day after Cortes entered the city and lasted for seven days.

On the third day, Motecuhzoma climbed onto the rooftop and tried to admonish his people, but they cursed him and shouted that he was a coward and a traitor to his country. They even threatened him with their weapons. It is said that an Indian killed him with a stone from his sling, but the palace servants declared that the Spaniards put him to death by stabbing him in the abdomen with their swords.

On the seventh day, the Spaniards abandoned the city along with the Tlaxcaltecas, the Huexotzincas and their other allies. They fled down the causeway that leads out to Tlacopan. But before they left, they murdered King Cacama of Tezcoco, his three sisters and two of his brothers.

There are several accounts by Indians who took part in the fighting that ensued. They tell how their warriors killed a great many of the Spaniards and their allies, and how the army took refuge on a mountain near Tlacopan and then marched to Tlaxcala.

[1] According to Bernal Diaz the Spaniards built only one bridge.

[2] Dugout canoes. The Aztecs had no vessels larger than the trees that could be carried down from the forests.

[3] A section of the island city. Tenochtitlan was the main section and gave the city its name.

[4] The portable bridge was left behind when the fury of the Aztec assault turned the Spanish retreat into a headlong flight.

[5] An obvious contradiction. The bridge had already been abandoned before the Spaniards reached the Canal of the Toltecs.

[6] The Tepanecas had been the dominant tribe in the Valley of Mexico about a hundred years before the Conquest, but they had been conquered by an alliance among the cities of Tenochtitlan, Tlacopan and Tezcoco, and had never regained any of their former power.

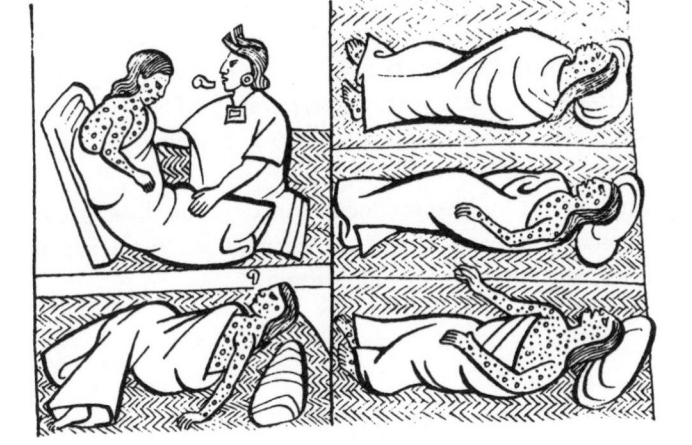

Chapter Eleven

The Siege of Tenochtitlan

Introduction

The Aztecs, convinced that the Spaniards would never return to Tenochtitlan, celebrated their fiestas again in the traditional manner, and Cuitlahuac was elected king to succeed his brother Motecuhzoma. The Aztec kings were chosen by a council of four lords, representing the four quarters, or phratries, into which the twenty clans of the city were evenly grouped. The council attempted to choose the wisest and bravest man among the brothers, sons and nephews of the previous ruler. Their choice of Cuitlahuac may have been influenced by the fact that he had warned against allowing the Spaniards to enter Tenochtitlan (Chapter 7).

This period of normalcy was soon ended by the terrible

plague that quickly spread through the city. The plague seems to have been an epidemic of smallpox, which was previously unknown among the Indians. One of its victims was the new king himself. Shortly afterward, the Spaniards reappeared. They had rebuilt their army in Tlaxcala and marched to Tlacopan by way of Tezcoco.

A number of indigenous documents describe the siege of the Aztec capital. We have chosen the account given by Sahagun's native informants in the *Codex Florentino.*

Tenochtitlan After the Departure of Cortes

When the Spaniards left Tenochtitlan, the Aztecs thought they had departed for good and would never return. Therefore they repaired and decorated the temple of their god, sweeping it clean and throwing out all the dirt and wreckage.

Then the eighth month[1] arrived, and the Aztecs celebrated it as always.[2] They adorned the impersonators of the gods, all those who played the part of gods in the ceremonies, decking them with necklaces and turquoise masks and dressing them in the sacred clothing. This clothing was made of quetzal feathers, eagle feathers and yellow parrot feathers. The finery of the gods was in the care of the great princes.

The Plague Ravages the City

While the Spaniards were in Tlaxcala, a great plague broke out here in Tenochtitlan. It began to spread during the thirteenth month[3] and lasted for seventy days, striking everywhere in the city and killing a vast number of our people. Sores erupted on our faces, our breasts, our bellies; we were covered with agonizing sores from head to foot.

The illness was so dreadful that no one could walk or move. The sick were so utterly helpless that they could only lie on their beds like corpses, unable to move their limbs or even their heads. They could not lie face down or roll from one side to the other. If they did move their bodies, they screamed with pain.

A great many died from this plague, and many others died of hunger. They could not get up to search for food, and everyone else was too sick to care for them, so they starved to death in their beds.

Some people came down with a milder form of the disease; they suffered less than the others and made a good recovery. But they could not escape entirely. Their looks were ravaged, for wherever a sore broke out, it gouged an ugly pockmark in the skin. And a few of the survivors were left completely blind.

The first cases were reported in Cuatlan. By the time the danger was recognized, the plague was so well established that nothing could halt it, and eventually it spread all the way to Chalco. Then its virulence diminished considerably, though there were isolated cases for many months after. The first victims were stricken during the fiesta of Teotlecco,[4] and the faces of our warriors were not clean and free of sores until the fiesta of Panquetzaliztli.[5]

The Spaniards Return

And now the Spaniards came back again. They marched here by way of Tezcoco, set up headquarters in Tlacopan and then divided their forces. Pedro de Alvarado was assigned the road to the Tlatelolco quarter as his personal responsibility, while Cortes himself took charge of the Coyoacan area and the road from Acachinanco to Tenochtitlan proper. Cortes knew that the captain of Tenochtitlan was extremely brave.

The first battle began outside Tlatelolco, either at the ash pits or at the place called the Point of the Alders, and then shifted to Nonohualco. Our warriors put the enemy to flight and not a single Aztec was killed. The Spaniards tried a second advance but our warriors attacked them from their boats, loosing such a storm of arrows that the Spaniards were forced to retreat again.

Cortes, however, set out for Acachinanco and reached his goal. He moved his headquarters there, just outside the city. Heavy fighting ensued, but the Aztecs could not dislodge him.

The Spaniards Launch Their Brigantines

Finally the ships, a dozen in all, came from Tezcoco[6] and anchored near Acachinanco. Cortes went out to inspect the canals that traversed the causeways, to discover the best passages for his fleet. He wanted to know which were the nearest, the shortest, the deepest, the straightest, so that none of his ships would run aground or be trapped inside. One of the canals across the Xoloco thoroughfare was so twisted and narrow that only two of the smaller ships were able to pass through it.

The Spaniards now decided to attack Tenochtitlan and destroy its people. The cannons were mounted in the ships, the sails were raised and the fleet moved out onto the lake. The flagship led the way, flying a great linen standard with Cortes' coat of arms. The soldiers beat their drums and blew their trumpets; they played their flutes and chirimias[7] and whistles.

Spanish Brigantines Besiege the City (Codex Florentino)

ninety-five

When the ships approached the Zoquiapan quarter,[8] the common people were terrified at the sight. They gathered their children into the canoes and fled helter-skelter across the lake, moaning with fear and paddling as swiftly as they could. They left all their possessions behind them and abandoned their little farms without looking back.

Our enemies seized all our possessions. They gathered up everything they could find and loaded it into the ships in great bundles. They stole our cloaks and blankets, our battle dress, our tabors and drums, and carried them all away. The Tlatelolcas followed and attacked the Spaniards from their boats but could not save any of the plunder.

When the Spaniards reached Xoloco, near the entrance to Tenochtitlan, they found that the Indians had built a wall across the road to block their progress. They destroyed it with four shots from the largest cannon. The first shot did little harm, but the second split it and the third opened a great hole. With the fourth shot, the wall lay in ruins on the ground.

Two of the brigantines, both with cannons mounted in their bows, attacked a flotilla of our shielded canoes. The cannons were fired into the thick of the flotilla, wherever the canoes were crowded closest together. Many of our warriors were killed outright; others drowned because they were too crippled by their wounds to swim away. The water was red with the blood of the dead and dying. Those who were hit by the steel arrows were also doomed; they died instantly and sank to the bottom of the lake.

Defensive Tactics of the Aztecs

When the Aztecs discovered that the shots from the arquebuses and cannons always flew in a straight line, they no longer ran away in the line of fire. They ran to the right or left or in zigzags, not in front of the guns. If they saw that a cannon was about to be fired and they could not escape by running, they threw themselves to the ground and lay flat until the shot had passed over them. The warriors also took cover among the houses, darting into the spaces between them. The road was suddenly as empty as if it passed through a desert.

Then the Spaniards arrived in Huitzillan,[9] where they found another wall blocking the road. A great crowd of our warriors was hiding behind it to escape the gunfire.

The Spaniards Debark

The brigantines came up and anchored nearby. They had been pursuing our war canoes in the open lake, but when they had almost run them down, they suddenly turned and sailed toward the causeway. Now they anchored a short distance from the houses. As soon as the cannons in their bows were loaded again, the soldiers aimed and fired them at the new wall.

The first shot cracked it in a dozen places, but it remained standing. They fired again: this time it cracked from one end to the other and crumpled to the ground. A moment later the road was completely empty. The warriors had all fled when they saw the wall collapsing; they ran blindly, this way and that, howling with fear.

Then the Spaniards debarked and filled in the canal. Working hurriedly, they threw in the stones from the shattered wall, the roof beams and adobe bricks from the nearest houses, anything they could find, until the surface of the fill was level with the causeway. Then a squad of about ten horsemen crossed over it. They galloped to and fro, scouting both sides of the road; they raced and wheeled and clattered back and forth. Soon they were joined by another squad that rode up to support them.

A number of Tlatelolcas had rushed into the palace where Motecuhzoma lived before he was slain. When they came out again, they unexpectedly met the Spanish cavalry. The lead horseman stabbed one of the Tlatelolcas, but the wounded man was able to clutch the lance and cling to it. His friends ran to his aid and twisted it from the Spaniard's hands. They knocked the horseman from his saddle, beat and kicked him as he lay on his back on the ground, and then cut off his head.

The Spaniards now joined all their forces into one unit and marched together as far as the Eagle Gate, where they set up the cannons they had brought with them. It was called the Eagle Gate because it was decorated with an enormous eagle carved of stone. The eagle was flanked on one side by a stone jaguar; on the other side there was a large honey bear, also of carved stone.

Two rows of tall columns led into the city from this gate. Some of the Aztecs hid behind the columns when they saw the Spaniards and their guns; others climbed onto the roofs of the communal houses. None of the warriors dared to show his face openly.

The Spaniards wasted no time as they loaded and fired the cannons. The smoke belched out in black clouds that darkened the sky, as if night were falling. The warriors hidden behind the columns broke from cover and fled; those on the rooftops climbed down and ran after them. When the smoke cleared away, the Spaniards could not see a single Aztec.

The Spaniards Advance to the Heart of the City

Then the Spaniards brought forward the largest cannon and set it up on the sacrificial stone. The priests of Huitzilopochtli immediately began to beat their great ritual drums from the top of the pyramid. The deep throbbing of the drums resounded over the city, calling the warriors to defend the shrine of their god. But two of the Spanish soldiers climbed the stairway to the temple platform, cut the priests down with their swords and pitched them headlong over the brink.

The great captains and warriors who had been fighting from their canoes now returned and landed. The canoes were paddled by the younger warriors and the recruits. As soon as the warriors landed, they ran through the streets, hunting the enemy and shouting: "Mexicanos, come find them!"

The Spaniards, seeing that an attack was imminent, tightened their ranks and clenched the hilts of their swords. The next moment, all was noise and confusion. The Aztecs charged into the plaza from every direction, and the air was black with arrows and gunsmoke.

The battle was so furious that both sides had to pull back. The Aztecs withdrew to Xoloco to catch their breath and dress their wounds, while the Spaniards retreated to their camp in Acachinanco, abandoning the cannon they had set up on the sacrificial stone. Later the warriors dragged this cannon to the edge of the canal and toppled it in. It sank at a place called the Stone Toad.

The Aztecs Take Refuge

During this time the Aztecs took refuge in the Tlatelolco quarter. They deserted the Tenochtitlan quarters all in one day, weeping and lamenting like women. Husbands searched for their wives, and fathers carried their small children on their shoulders. Tears of grief and despair streamed down their cheeks.

The Tlatelolcas, however, refused to give up.[10] They raced into Tenochtitlan to continue the fight and the Spaniards soon learned how brave they were. Pedro de Alvarado launched an attack against the Point of the Alders, in the direction of Nonohualco, but his troops were shattered as if he had sent them against a stone cliff. The battle was fought both on dry land and on the water, where the Indians shot at the Spaniards from their shielded canoes. Alvarado was routed and had to draw back to Tlacopan.

On the following day, two brigantines came up loaded with troops, and the Spaniards united all their forces on the outskirts of Nonohualco. The soldiers in the brigantines came ashore and the whole army marched into the very heart of Tenochtitlan. Wherever they went, they found the streets empty, with no Indians anywhere in sight.

The Last Stand

Then the great captain Tzilacatzin arrived, bringing with him three large, round stones of the kind used for building walls. He carried one of them in his hand; the other two hung from his shield. When he hurled these stones at the Spaniards, they turned and fled the city.

Tzilacatzin's military rank was that of Otomi, and he clipped his hair in the style of the Otomies.[11] He scorned his enemies, Spaniards as well as Indians; they all shook with terror at the mere sight of him.

one hundred

When the Spaniards found out how dangerous he was, they tried desperately to kill him. They attacked him with their swords and spears, fired at him with their crossbows and arquebuses, and tried every other means they could think of to kill or cripple him. Therefore he wore various disguises to prevent them from recognizing him.

Sometimes he wore his lip plug, his gold earrings and all the rest of his full regalia, but left his head uncovered to show that he was an Otomi. At other times he wore only his cotton armor, with a thin kerchief wrapped around his head. At still other times, he put on the finery of the priests who cast the victims into the fire: [12] a plumed headdress with the eagle symbol on its crest, and gleaming gold bracelets on both arms, and circular bands of gleaming gold on both ankles.

The Spaniards came back again the next day. They brought their ships to a point just off Nonohualco, close to the place called the House of Mist. Their other troops arrived on foot, along with the Tlaxcaltecas. As soon as they had formed ranks, they charged the Aztec warriors.

The heaviest fighting began when they entered Nonohualco. None of our enemies and none of our own warriors escaped harm. Everyone was wounded, and the toll of the dead was grievous on both sides. The struggle continued all day and all night.

Only three captains never retreated. They were contemptuous of their enemies and gave no thought whatever to their own safety. The first of these heroes was Tzoyectzin; the second, Temoctzin; and the third, the great Tzilacatzin.

At last the Spaniards were too exhausted to keep on fighting. After one final attempt to break the Aztec ranks, they withdrew to their camp to rest and recover, with their allies trailing behind.

[1] Corresponding to June 22–July 11 in our calendar. The Aztec year was divided into eighteen months (group of twenty days) plus five unlucky days called *nemontemi*.

[2] The first day of the eighth month was the fiesta of Huixtocihuatl, goddess of salt.

[3] September 30–October 19.

[4] The twelfth month, September 10–29.

[5] The fifteenth month, November 9–28.

[6] These vessels were built in Tlaxcala, dismantled, carried piece by piece to Lake Tezcoco, then put together again and launched. The sails, rigging and ironwork were brought from the Gulf coast, where they had been stored since the march inland. Cortes ordered the fleet built because the disastrous Night of Sorrows had taught him the danger of using the causeways without having domination of the lake.

[7] Double-reed woodwinds, similar to shepherd's pipes; precursors of the modern oboe.

[8] In the southwestern section of the island city.

[9] Closer to Tenochtitlan than Xoloco, on the same avenue.

[10] Although Tlatelolco had become a part of Tenochtitlan by the time of the Conquest, it had once been an independent city and still retained its name and its local pride. The majority of Sahagun's informants were Tlatelolcas, and in this passage they may be glorifying their home quarter at the expense of Tenochtitlan proper.

[11] See Chapter 5, note 1.

[12] In the ceremony honoring the fire god, Huehueteotl, bound captives were hurled into a great bonfire. Before they could die, the priests dragged them out with hooks, cut open their chests and tore out their hearts.

Chapter Twelve

Spanish Raids into the Besieged City

Introduction

The native documents describing the long siege of Tenochtitlan present a number of vivid and dramatic scenes. We have selected the account by Sahagun's informants preserved in the *Codex Florentino*.

During one of the first attacks by the Spaniards, the Aztecs took fifteen prisoners and then sacrificed them within sight of their comrades, who were watching helplessly from the barkentines. The text also describes the tragic suffering of the besieged inhabitants, the Spanish raid on the Tlatelolco market place, the burning of the temple, and the almost incredible courage with which the Aztecs again and again drove back the invaders.

The narrative continues with a description of how the

Spaniards set up a catapult on the platform of the small temple in the Tlatelolco market, and concludes with the final efforts of the Aztecs to save their capital. Cuauhtemoc, who had succeeded his uncle Cuitlahuac when the latter died of the plague, decided to dress a captain named Opochtzin in the regalia of King Ahuitzotl, Motecuhzoma's predecessor. It was believed that this regalia invested its wearer with the attributes of the war god Huitzilopochtli, and that if Opochtzin could wound a Spaniard with the sacred arrow called "the fire-serpent," victory was still possible. The attempt was unsuccessful and was followed by a brief period of calm that ended with the final agonies of the dying city.

Fifteen Spaniards Are Captured and Sacrificed

The warriors advanced to the sound of flutes. They shouted their war cries and beat their shields like drums. They pursued the Spaniards, harried and terrified them, and at last took fifteen of them prisoners. The rest of the Spaniards retreated to their ships and sailed out into the middle of the lake.

The prisoners were sacrificed in the place called Tlacochcalco [House of the Arsenal]. Their captors quickly plundered them, seizing their weapons, their cotton armor and everything else, until they stood naked. Then they were sacrificed to the god, while their comrades on the lake watched them being put to death.

Two of the barkentines sailed to Xocotitlan again. They anchored there, and the Spaniards began attacking the houses along the shore. But when Tzilacatzin and other warriors saw what was happening, they ran to the defense and drove the invaders into the water.

On another occasion, the barkentines approached Coyonacazco to attack the houses. As the ships closed in, a few Spaniards jumped out, ready for battle. They were led by Castaneda and by Xicotencatl, who was wearing his headdress of quetzal feathers.

Then Castaneda shot the catapult.[1] It struck one of the Aztecs in the forehead and he fell dead where he was standing. The warriors charged the Spaniards, driving them into the water, and then loosed a hail of stones from their slings. Castaneda would have been killed in this action if a barkentine had not taken him aboard and sailed away toward Xocotitlan.

Another barkentine was anchored near the turn in the wall, and still another near Teotlecco, where the road runs straight to Tepetzinco. They were stationed as guards in order to control the lake. They sailed away that night, but after a few days they came back again to their stations.

The Spaniards advanced from the direction of Cuahuecatitlan. Their allies from Tlaxcala, Acolhuacan and Chalco filled up the canal[2] so that the army could pass. They threw in adobe bricks and all the woodwork of the nearby houses: the lintels, the doorjambs, the beams and pillars. They even threw canestalks and rushes into the water.

The Spaniards Attack Again

When the canal had been filled up, the Spaniards marched over it. They advanced cautiously, with their standard-bearer in the lead, and they beat their drums and played their chirimias as they came. The Tlaxcaltecas and the other allies followed close behind. The Tlaxcaltecas held their heads high and pounded their breasts with their hands, hoping to frighten us with their arrogance and courage. They sang songs as they marched, but the Aztecs were also singing. It was as if both sides were challenging each other with their songs. They sang whatever they happened to remember and the music strengthened their hearts.

The Aztec warriors hid when the enemy reached solid ground. They crouched down to make themselves as small as possible and waited for the signal, the shout that told them it was the moment to stand up and attack. Suddenly they heard it: "Mexicanos, now is the time!"

The captain Hecatzin leaped up and raced toward the Spaniards, shouting: "Warriors of Tlatelolco, now is the time! Who are these barbarians? Let them come ahead!" He attacked one of the Spaniards and knocked him to the ground, but the Spaniard also managed to knock Hecatzin down. The captain got up and clubbed the Spaniard again, and other warriors rushed forward to drag him away.

Then all the Aztecs sprang up and charged into battle. The Spaniards were so astonished that they blundered here and there like drunkards; they ran through the streets with the warriors in pursuit. This was when the taking of captives began. A great many of the allies from Tlaxcala, Acolhuacan, Chalco and Xochimilco were overpowered by the Aztecs, and there was a great harvesting of prisoners, a great reaping of victims to be sacrificed.

The Spaniards and their allies waded into the lake because the road had become too slippery for them. The mud was so slick that they sprawled and floundered and could not stand up to fight. The Aztecs seized them as captives and dragged them across the mud.

The Spanish standard was taken and carried off during this encounter. The warriors from Tlatelolco captured it in the place known today as San Martin, but they were scornful of their prize and considered it of little importance.

Some of the Spaniards were able to escape with their lives. They retreated in the direction of Culhuacan, on the edge of the canal, and gathered there to recover their strength.

Fifty-three Spaniards Are Sacrificed

The Aztecs took their prisoners to Yacacolco, hurrying them along the road under the strictest guard. Some of the captives were weeping, some were keening, and others were beating their palms against their mouths.

When they arrived in Yacacolco, they were lined up in long rows. One by one they were forced to climb to the temple platform, where they were sacrificed by the priests. The Spaniards went first, then their allies, and all were put to death.

As soon as the sacrifices were finished, the Aztecs ranged the Spaniards' heads in rows on pikes. They also lined up their horses' heads. They placed the horses' heads at the bottom and the heads of the Spaniards above, and arranged them all so that the faces were toward the sun. However, they did not display any of the allies' heads. All told, fifty-three Spaniards and four horses were sacrificed there in Yacacolco.

The fighting continued in many different places. At one point, the allies from Xochimilco surrounded us in their canoes, and the toll of the dead and captured was heavy on both sides.

The Sufferings of the Inhabitants

The Spanish blockade caused great anguish in the city. The people were tormented by hunger, and many starved to

Heads of Spaniards and Horses Sacrificed by the Aztecs
(Codex Florentino)

one hundred and eight

death. There was no fresh water to drink,[3] only stagnant water and the brine of the lake,[4] and many people died of dysentery.

The only food was lizards, swallows, corncobs and the salt grasses of the lake. The people also ate water lilies and the seeds of the colorin,[5] and chewed on deerhides and pieces of leather. They roasted and seared and scorched whatever they could find and then ate it. They ate the bitterest weeds and even dirt.

Nothing can compare with the horrors of that siege and the agonies of the starving. We were so weakened by hunger that, little by little, the enemy forced us to retreat. Little by little they forced us to the wall.

The Battle in the Market Place

On one occasion, four Spanish cavalrymen entered the market place. They rode through it in a great circle, stabbing and killing many of our warriors and trampling everything under their horses' hooves. This was the first time the Spaniards had entered the market place, and our warriors were taken by surprise. But when the horsemen withdrew, the warriors recovered their wits and ran in pursuit.

It was at this same time that the Spaniards set fire to the temple and burned it to the ground. The flames and smoke leaped high into the air with a terrible roar. The people wept when they saw their temple on fire; they wept and cried out, fearing that afterward it would be plundered.

The battle lasted for many hours and extended to almost every corner of the market place. There was no action along the wall where the vendors sold lime, but the fighting raged among the flower stalls, and the stalls offering snails, and all the passageways between them.

Some of our warriors stationed themselves on the rooftops of the Quecholan district, which is near the entrance to the market place, and from there they hurled stones and fired arrows at the enemy. Others broke holes in the rear walls of all the houses of Quecholan, holes just big enough for a man's body to pass through. When the cavalry attacked and were about to spear our warriors, or trample them, or cut off their retreat, they slipped through the holes and the mounted men could not follow.

Other Battles

On another occasion the Spaniards entered Atliyacapan. They ransacked the houses and captured a number of prisoners, but when the warriors saw what was happening, they loosed their arrows and rushed forward to attack. The leader of this attack, a valiant chief named Axoquentzin, pressed the enemy so hard that they were forced to release their prisoners and drop all their spoils. But this great chief died when a Spanish sword entered his breast and found his heart.

There were other battles in Yacacolco, where the enemy killed many of the Aztecs with their crossbows. The warriors drew back and tried to waylay the rear guard, but a few of the allies saw them and climbed to the rooftops. They cried: "Warriors of Tlaxcala, come here! Your enemies are here!" The Tlaxcaltecas shot so many arrows at the men in ambush that they had to break and run.

Later in the day, the Aztecs put up a much stronger resistance, and the Spaniards and their allies could not break their ranks. The Tlatelolcas took up positions on the opposite side of the canal, hurling stones and shooting arrows across it. The enemy could not advance or capture any of the bridges.

The Catapult Is Set Up in the Market Place

During this time, the Spaniards mounted a wooden catapult on the temple platform to fling stones at the Indians. While it was being set up, the Indians who had gathered in Amaxac came out to stare at it. They pointed at the machine and asked each other what it could be. When the Spaniards had finished their preparations and were ready to shoot it at the crowd, they wound it up until the wooden beams stood erect. Then they released it like a great sling.

But the stone did not fall among the Indians. It flew over their heads and crashed into a corner of the market place. This seemed to cause an argument among the Spaniards: they gestured toward the Indians and shouted at each other. But still they could not aim the machine correctly. It threw out its stones in every direction.

Finally the Indians were able to see how it worked: it had a sling inside it, worked by a heavy rope. The Indians named it "the wooden sling."

The Spaniards and Tlaxcaltecas retreated again, marching back to Yacacolco and Tecpancaltitlan in closed ranks. Their leader was directing the campaign against us from his headquarters in Acocolecan.

The Aztec Defense

Our warriors rallied to defend the city. Their spirits and courage were high; not one of them showed any fear or behaved like a woman. They cried: "Mexicanos, come here and join us! Who are these savages? A mere rabble from the south!"[6] They did not move in a direct line; they moved in a zigzag course, never in a straight line.

The Spanish soldiers often disguised themselves so that they would not be recognized. They wore cloaks like those of the Aztecs and put on the same battle dress and adornments, hoping to deceive our warriors into thinking they were not Spaniards.

Whenever the Aztecs saw the enemy notching their arrows, they either dispersed or flattened themselves on the ground. The warriors of Tlatelolco were very alert; they were very cautious and vigilant, and watched intently to see where the shots were coming from.

But step by step the Spaniards gained more ground and captured more houses. They forced us backward along the Amaxac road with their spears and shields.

The Quetzal-Owl

Cuauhtemoc consulted with a group of his captains and then called in a great captain named Opochtzin, who was a dyer by trade. They dressed him in the finery of the Quetzal-Owl, which had belonged to King Ahuitzotl.[7] Then Cuauhtemoc said to him: "This regalia belonged to my father, the great warrior Ahuitzotl. Terrify our enemies with it. Annihilate our enemies with it. Let them behold it and tremble."

The king ordered four captains to go with Opochtzin as a rear guard. He placed in the captain's hands the magic object that was the most important part of the regalia. This was an arrow with a long shaft and an obsidian tip.

The captain Tlacotzin said: "Mexicanos, the power of Huitzilopochtli resides in this finery. Loose the sacred arrow at our enemies, for it is the Serpent of Fire, the Arrow that Pierces the Fire. Loose it at the invaders; drive them away with the power of Huitzilopochtli. But shoot it straight and well, for it must not fall to earth. And if it should wound one or two of our foes, then we shall still have a little time left and a chance to conquer them. Now, let us see what the god's will may be!"

The Quetzal-Owl departed with the four captains, and the quetzal feathers seemed to open out, making him appear even greater and more terrifying. When our enemies saw him approach, they quaked as if they thought a mountain were about to fall on them. They trembled with dread, as if they knew the finery could work magic.

The Quetzal-Owl climbed up onto a rooftop. When our enemies saw him, they came forward and prepared to attack him, but he succeeded in driving them away. Then he came down from the rooftop with his quetzal feathers and his gold ornaments. He was not killed in this action and our enemies could not capture the feathers or the gold. Three of the enemy soldiers were taken prisoner.

Suddenly the battle ended. Neither side moved against the other; the night was calm and silent, with no incidents of any kind. On the following day, absolutely nothing took place, and neither the Spaniards nor the Indians spoke a word. The Indians waited in their defense works, and the Spaniards waited in their positions. Each side watched the other closely but made no plans for launching an attack. Both sides passed the whole day in this fashion, merely watching and waiting.

[1] Described later in the following text.
[2] Which intersected the causeway.
[3] The Spaniards had broken the aqueduct that brought fresh water to the city from Chapultepec on the mainland.

one hundred and thirteen

[4] The lake water was saline except at the extreme south, around Xochimilco and Chalco.

[5] *Erythrina americana.*

[6] In Aztec religious geography, the south was sometimes the region of disorder.

[7] Motecuhzoma's uncle and predecessor.

Chapter Thirteen

The Surrender of Tenochtitlan

Introduction

The texts in this chapter have been taken from three different indigenous sources. The first selection, by Sahagun's native informants, describes a final omen that presaged the imminent destruction of the Aztec capital. According to this account, it was Cuauhtemoc himself who surrendered Tenochtitlan to the Spaniards. The informants also give an eloquent description of the tragic scenes that accompanied the taking of the city.

The second selection is from the *XII relacion* by Alva Ixtlilxochitl. Its most memorable passage is the moment when Cuauhtemoc was brought face to face with Cortes. The king placed his hand on the conquistador's dagger and begged him to kill him with it, since he had already destroyed the kingdom.

The last selection is from the *VII relacion* by Chimalpain, and was translated from Nahuatl to Spanish by Miguel Leon-Portilla. It describes how Cortes bullied and even tortured the Aztec lords in order to obtain the gold and other valuables that the Indians had treasured since ancient times.

The Final Omen

(From the *Codex Florentino* by Sahagun's informants)

At nightfall it began to rain, but it was more like a heavy dew than a rain. Suddenly the omen appeared, blazing like a great bonfire in the sky. It wheeled in enormous spirals like a whirlwind and gave off a shower of sparks and red-hot coals, some great and some little. It also made loud noises, rumbling and hissing like a metal tube placed over a fire. It circled the wall nearest the lakeshore and then hovered for a while above Coyonacazco. From there it moved out into the middle of the lake, where it suddenly disappeared. No one cried out when this omen came into view: the people knew what it meant and they watched it in silence.

Nothing whatever occurred on the following day. Our warriors and the Spanish soldiers merely waited in their positions. Cortes kept a constant watch, standing under a many-colored canopy on the roof of the lord Aztautzin's house, which is near Amaxac. His officers stood around him, talking among themselves.

Cuauhtemoc's Surrender

The Aztec leaders gathered in Tolmayecan to discuss what they should do. Cuauhtemoc and the other nobles tried to determine how much tribute they would have to pay and how best to surrender to the strangers. Then the nobles put Cuauhtemoc into a war canoe, with only three men to accompany him: a captain named Teputztitloloc, a servant named Iaztachimal and a boatman named Cenyautl. When the people saw their chief departing, they wept and cried out: "Our youngest prince is leaving us! He is going to surrender to the Spaniards! He is going to surrender to the 'gods'!"

The Spaniards came out to meet him. They took him by the hand, led him up to the rooftop and brought him into the presence of Cortes. The Captain stared at him for a moment and then patted him on the head. Then he gestured toward a chair and the two leaders sat down side by side.

The Spaniards began to shoot off their cannons, but they were not trying to hit anyone. They merely loaded and fired, and the cannonballs flew over the Indians' heads. Later they put one of the cannons into a boat and took it to the house of Coyohuehuetzin, where they hoisted it to the rooftop.

The Flight from the City

Once again the Spaniards started killing and a great many Indians died. The flight from the city began and with this the war came to an end. The people cried: "We have suffered enough! Let us leave the city! Let us go live on weeds!" Some fled across the lake, others along the causeways, and even then there were many killings. The Spaniards were angry because our warriors still carried their shields and *macanas*.[1]

Those who lived in the center of the city went straight toward Amaxac, to the fork in the road. From there they fled

one hundred and seventeen

in various directions, some toward Tepeyacac, others toward Xoxohuiltitlan and Nonohualco; but no one went toward Xoloco or Mazatzintamalco. Those who lived in boats or on the wooden rafts anchored in the lake fled by water, as did the inhabitants of Tolmayecan. Some of them waded in water up to their chests and even up to their necks. Others drowned when they reached water above their heads.

The grownups carried their young children on their shoulders. Many of the children were weeping with terror, but a few of them laughed and smiled, thinking it was great sport to be carried like that along the road.

Some of the people who owned canoes departed in the daytime, but the others, the majority, left by night. They almost crashed into each other in their haste as they paddled away from the city.

The Spaniards Humiliate the Refugees

The Spanish soldiers were stationed along the roads to search the fleeing inhabitants. They were looking only for gold and paid no attention to jade, turquoise or quetzal feathers. The women carried their gold under their skirts and the men carried it in their mouths or under their loincloths. Some of the women, knowing they would be searched if they looked prosperous, covered their faces with mud and dressed themselves in rags. They put on rags for skirts and rags for blouses; everything they wore was in tatters. But the Spaniards searched all the women without exception: those with light skins, those with dark skins, those with dark bodies.

A few of the men were separated from the others. These

ycpolinhõmexnca

Surrender of the Aztecs (Lienzo de Tlaxcala)

one hundred and nineteen

men were the bravest and strongest warriors, the warriors with manly hearts. The youths who served them were also told to stand apart. The Spaniards immediately branded them with hot irons, either on the cheek or the lips.

The day on which we laid down our shields and admitted defeat was the day 1-Serpent in the year 3-House.[2] When Cuauhtemoc surrendered, the Spaniards hurried him to Acachinanco at night, but on the following day, just after sunrise, many of them came back again. They were dressed for battle, with their coats of mail and their metal helmets, but they had left their swords and shields behind. They all tied white handkerchiefs over their noses because they were sickened by the stench of the rotting bodies. They came back on foot, dragging Cuauhtemoc, Coanacotzin and Tetlepanquetzaltzin by their cloaks.

Cortes Demands Gold

When the fighting had ended, Cortes demanded the gold his men had abandoned in the Canal of the Toltecs during the Night of Sorrows. He called the chiefs together and asked them: "Where is the gold you were hiding in the city?"

The Aztecs unloaded it from canoes: there were bars of gold, gold crowns, gold ornaments for the arms and legs, gold helmets and disks of gold. They heaped it in front of the Captain, and the Spaniards came forward to take possession of it. Cortes said: "Is this all the gold in the city? You must bring me all of it."

Tlacotzin replied: "I beg the lord to hear me. All the gold we owned was kept in our palaces. Is it not true that our lords took all of it with them?"

La Malinche told Cortes what Tlacotzin had said. Then she translated the Captain's answer: "Yes, it is true. We took it and stamped it with our seal. But we lost it in the Canal of the Toltecs when your warriors surprised us. You must bring it all back."

Tlacotzin replied: "I beg the god to hear me. The people of Tenochtitlan do not know how to fight in canoes; it is not their custom. This is done only by the people of Tlatelolco, who fought in canoes to defend themselves from your attacks. Is it not possible that the Tlatelolcas took the gold?"

Then Cuauhtemoc said to Tlacotzin: "Yes, it is very possible. Our lords may have taken the wrong people prisoners. Everything suggests it. The rest of the gold must be in Texopan. The gold our lords took is here." Cuauhtemoc pointed at the heap they had unloaded from the canoes.

The Captain replied: "Only this little?"

Tlacotzin said: "Perhaps someone has stolen the rest. Why not search for it? Why not bring it to light?"

La Malinche told him what the Captain replied: "You must bring us two hundred bars of gold of this size." And she held her hands apart to show them the size.

Tlacotzin said: "Perhaps some woman has hidden the gold under her skirts. Why not search for it? Why not bring it to light?"

Ahuelitoc the Mixcoatlailotlac said: "I beg our lord and master to hear me. Even as late as the reign of Motecuhzoma, the Tepanecas[3] and the Acolhuas joined the people of Tenochtitlan and Tlatelolco in conquering our enemies.[4] We all went out together to defeat them; and when they had surrendered, we each went back to our own city. Then the conquered tribes brought us the tribute we had imposed: quetzal feathers, gold, jade, turquoise and other kinds of precious stones, as well as birds with rich plumage, such as the bluejay and the bird with a crimson ruff. All these things were brought here to Tenochtitlan: all the tribute, all the gold...."

The Ravage of Tenochtitlan

(From the *XII relacion* by Alva Ixtilxochitl)

On the day that Tenochtitlan was taken, the Spaniards committed some of the most brutal acts ever inflicted upon the unfortunate people of this land. The cries of the helpless women and children were heart-rending. The Tlaxcaltecas and the other enemies of the Aztecs revenged themselves pitilessly for old offenses and robbed them of everything they could find. Only Prince Ixtlilxochitl of Tezcoco, ally of Cortes, felt compassion for the Aztecs, because they were of his own homeland. He kept his followers from maltreating the women and children as cruelly as did Cortes and the Spaniards.

At nightfall the invading forces retired again. Prince Ixtlilxochitl, Cortes and the other captains agreed to complete the conquest of the city on the following day, the day of St. Hippolytus the Martyr.[5] Shortly after daybreak, they approached the place where the remnants of the enemy were gathered. Cortes marched through the streets, but Ixtlilxochitl and Sandoval, the captain of the brigantines, approached by water. Ixtlilxochitl had been informed that Cuauhtemoc and his followers were assembling for escape in their canoes.

The anguish and bewilderment of our foes was pitiful to see. The warriors gathered on the rooftops and stared at the ruins of their city in a dazed silence, and the women and children and old men were all weeping. The lords and nobles crowded into the canoes with their king.

The Capture of Cuauhtemoc

At a given signal, our forces attacked the enemy all at once. We pressed forward so swiftly that within a few hours we had totally defeated them. Our brigantines and canoes attacked their flotilla; they could not withstand us but scattered in every direction, with our forces pursuing them. Garcia de Olguin, who commanded one of the brigantines, was told by an Aztec prisoner that the canoe he was following was that of the king. He bore down on it and gradually caught up with it.

Cuauhtemoc, seeing that the enemy was overtaking him, ordered the boatman to turn the canoe toward our barkentine and prepare to attack it. He grasped his shield and *macana* and was determined to give battle. But when he realized that the enemy could overwhelm him with crossbows and muskets, he put down his arms and surrendered.

Cuauhtemoc Acknowledges His Defeat

Garcia de Olguin brought him before Cortes, who received him with all the respect due to a king. Cuauhtemoc placed his hand on the Captain's dagger and said: "I have done everything in my power to save my kingdom from your hands. Since fortune has been against me, I now beg you to take my life. This would put an end to the kingship of Mexico, and it would be just and right, for you have already destroyed my city and killed my people." He spoke other grief-stricken words, which touched the heart of everyone who heard them.

Cortes consoled him and asked him to command his warriors to surrender. Cuauhtemoc immediately climbed onto a high tower and shouted to them to cease fighting, for everything had fallen to the enemy. Of the 300,000 warriors who had defended the city, 60,000 were left. When they heard their king, they laid down their arms and the nobles came forward to comfort him.

Ixtlilxochitl was eager to clasp Cuauhtemoc's hand. The prince arrived in one of the two brigantines that were taking various lords and ladies to Cortes; among these were Tlacahuepantzin, son of Motecuhzoma, and Queen Papantzin Oxomoc, widow of Cuitlahuac. Ixtlilxochitl led them into the Captain's presence. Then he ordered that the queen and the other ladies be taken to Tezcoco and held there under guard.

That same day, after looting the city, the Spaniards apportioned all the gold and silver among themselves, leaving the feathers and precious stones for the nobles of Tezcoco and the cloaks and other objects for their warriors.

The Length of the Siege

The siege of Tenochtitlan, according to the histories, paintings and chronicles, lasted exactly eighty days. Thirty thousand men from the kingdom of Tezcoco were killed during this time, of the more than 200,000 who fought on the side of the Spaniards. Of the Aztecs, more than 240,000 were killed. Almost all of the nobility perished: there remained alive only a few lords and knights and the little children.

Cortes Deals with the Nobles and Priests

(From the *VII relacion* by Chimalpain)

When the arms and trappings of war had been put aside,

the lords were brought together in Acachinanco. These were Cuauhtemoc, lord of Tenochtitlan; Tlacotzin, the serpent woman;[6] Oquiztzin, lord of Azcapotzalco; Panitzin, lord of Ecatepec; and Motelhuihtzin, the royal steward. The last-named was not a prince, but he was a great captain during the war. Cortes ordered that they be bound and taken to Coyoacan. Panitzin, however, was not bound. At Coyoacan they were thrown into prison, where the Spaniards burned their feet.

It was at this same time that the Spaniards questioned the priests Cuauhcoatl, Cohuayhuitl, Tecohuentzin and Tetlanmecatl about the gold that had been lost in the Canal of the Toltecs. The Spaniards also demanded the eight bars of gold that had been stored in the palace under the care of the steward Ocuitecatl. The steward had died of smallpox during the plague. Only his son was left; and when he discovered that four of the eight bars had disappeared, he immediately fled.

The five lords who had been taken to Coyoacan were led from the prison, and Cortes addressed them through his interpreters, Jeronimo de Aguilar and La Malinche: "I want to know who the rulers of the city were, and also who ruled the Tepanecas and the people of Acolhuacan, Chalco and Xochimilco."

The five lords deliberated for a while. Then Tlacotzin said: "I beg the god to hear these few words of mine. I had no lands whatever when I first came here; the Tepanecas, the Acolhuas and the people of Chalco and Xochimilco all had lands. I made myself their lord with arrows and shields, and took possession of their lands. But what I did was no more than what you have done, for you also have come here with arrows and shields to capture all our cities."

When the Captain heard this, he turned to the other lords, and spoke in a voice ringing with authority: "He came here with arrows and shields to seize your lands. He forced you to be his servants. But now that I have come, I set you free. You are no longer his vassals. Your lands are your own again."

[1] The *macana* was a sort of flattened club edged with sharp pieces of obsidian. It was the dreaded closing-in weapon of the Aztec warrior.

[2] August 13, 1521.

[3] See Chapter 10, note 6.

[4] There was a triple alliance among the Aztecs, the Tepanecas of Tacuba and the Acolhuas of Tezcoco. Motecuhzoma, King of Mexico around 1440, became the leader of the allied armies, conquering towns and small states in what is today Guerrero and Morelos.

[5] August 13, 1521.

[6] See Chapter 3, note 1. Tlilpotonque, who held this office under Motecuhzoma, had apparently died in battle or in the siege.

Chapter Fourteen

The Story of the Conquest as Told by the Anonymous Authors of Tlatelolco

Introduction

In the thirteen preceding chapters we have presented the story of the Conquest in selections from various native sources, arranged according to the chronological sequence of events. Now, as a recapitulation, we offer another indigenous account. It describes all the major incidents of the Conquest in briefer form, but it also contains a considerable amount of material that cannot be found in other documents. Therefore it is not a mere summary but an important, independent narrative. As such, it inevitably introduces a number of discrepancies, both with the texts we have presented earlier and with the Spanish chronicles of Bernal Diaz and others. This account was written in Nahuatl in 1528 by anonymous authors in Tlatelolco. Like several of the texts by Sahagun's native informants, it reflects the pride of the Tlatelolcas in their home quarter of the city. It is probably the oldest prose document of all those drawn upon in this book. The original is now in the National Library in Paris, where it forms part of *Unos anales historicos de la nacion mexicana*—the so-called Manuscript 22.

The Arrival of Cortes

Year 13-Rabbit. The Spaniards were sighted off the coast.

Year 1-Canestalk. The Spaniards came to the palace at Tlayacac. When the Captain arrived at the palace, Motecuhzoma sent the Cuetlaxteca[1] to greet him and to bring him two suns as gifts. One of these suns was made of the yellow metal, the other of the white.[2] The Cuetlaxteca also brought him a mirror to be hung on his person, a gold collar, a great gold pitcher, fans and ornaments of quetzal feathers and a shield inlaid with mother-of-pearl.

The envoys made sacrifices in front of the Captain. At this, he grew very angry. When they offered him blood in an "eagle dish," he shouted at the man who offered it and struck him with his sword. The envoys departed at once.

All the gifts which the Cuetlaxteca brought to the Captain were sent by Motecuhzoma. That is why the Cuetlaxteca went to meet the Captain at Tlayacac: he was only performing his duties as a royal envoy.

Then the Captain marched to Tenochtitlan. He arrived here during the month called Bird,[3] under the sign of the day

8-Wind. When he entered the city, we gave him chickens, eggs, corn, tortillas and drink. We also gave him firewood, and fodder for his "deer." Some of these gifts were sent by the lord of Tenochtitlan, the rest by the lord of Tlatelolco. Later the Captain marched back to the coast, leaving Don Pedro de Alvarado—The Sun—in command.

The Massacre in the Main Temple

During this time, the people asked Motecuhzoma how they should celebrate their god's fiesta. He said: "Dress him in all his finery, in all his sacred ornaments."

During this same time, The Sun commanded that Motecuhzoma and Itzcohuatzin, the military chief of Tlatelolco, be made prisoners. The Spaniards hanged a chief from Acolhuacan named Nezahualquentzin. They also murdered the king of Nauhtla, Cohualpopocatzin, by wounding him with arrows and then burning him alive.

For this reason, our warriors were on guard at the Eagle Gate. The sentries from Tenochtitlan stood at one side of the gate, and the sentries from Tlatelolco at the other. But messengers came to tell them to dress the figure of Huitzilopochtli. They left their posts and went to dress him in his sacred finery: his ornaments and his paper clothing.

When this had been done, the celebrants began to sing their songs. That is how they celebrated the first day of the fiesta. On the second day they began to sing again, but without warning they were all put to death. The dancers and singers were completely unarmed. They brought only their embroidered cloaks, their turquoises, their lip plugs, their necklaces,

one hundred and twenty-nine

An Incident During the Conquest (Codex Vaticanus A.)

one hundred and thirty

their clusters of heron feathers, their trinkets made of deer hooves. Those who played the drums, the old men, had brought their gourds of snuff and their timbrels. The Spaniards attacked the musicians first, slashing at their hands and faces until they had killed all of them. The singers—and even the spectators—were also killed. This slaughter in the Sacred Patio went on for three hours. Then the Spaniards burst into the rooms of the temple to kill the others: those who were carrying water, or bringing fodder for the horses, or grinding meal, or sweeping, or standing watch over this work.

The king Motecuhzoma, who was accompanied by Itzcohuatzin and by those who had brought food for the Spaniards, protested: "Our lords, that is enough! What are you doing? These people are not carrying shields or *macanas*. Our lords, they are completely unarmed!"

The Sun treacherously murdered our people on the twentieth day after the Captain left for the coast. We allowed the Captain to return to the city in peace. But on the following day we attacked him with all our might, and that was the beginning of the war.

The Night of Sorrows

The Spaniards attempted to slip out of the city at night, but we attacked furiously at the Canal of the Toltecs, and many of them died. This took place during the fiesta of Tecuilhuitl. The survivors gathered first at Mazatzintamalco and waited for the stragglers to come up.

Year 2-Flint. This was the year in which Motecuhzoma died. Itzcohuatzin of Tlatelolco died at the same time.

The Spaniards took refuge in Acueco, but they were driven out by our warriors. They fled to Teuhcalhueyacan and from there to Zoltepec. Then they marched through Citlaltepec and camped in Temazcalapan, where the people gave them hens, eggs and corn. They rested for a short while and marched on to Tlaxcala.

Soon after, an epidemic broke out in Tenochtitlan. Almost the whole population suffered from racking coughs and painful, burning sores.

The Spaniards Return

When the epidemic had subsided a little, the Spaniards marched out of Tlaxcala. The first place they attacked and conquered was Tepeyacac. They departed from there during the fiesta of Tlahuano, and they arrived in Tlapechhuan during the fiesta of Izcalli. Twenty days later they marched to Tezcoco, where they remained for forty days. Then they reached Tlacopan and established themselves in the palace.

There was no fighting of any kind while they were in Tlacopan. At the end of a week they all marched back to Tezcoco.

Eighty days later they went to Huaxtepec and Cuauhnahuac,⁴ and from there they attacked Xochimilco. A great many Tlatelolcas died in that battle. Then the Spaniards returned to Tezcoco again.

Year 3-House. The Aztecs began to fight among themselves. The princes Tzihuacpopocatzin and Cicpatzin Tecuecuenotzin were put to death, as were Axayaca and Xoxopehualoc, the sons of Motecuhzoma. These princes were killed because they tried to persuade the people to bring corn, hens and eggs to the Spaniards. They were killed by the priests, captains and elder brothers.

But the great chiefs were angry at these executions. They said to the murderers: "Have we ourselves become assassins? Only sixty days ago, our people were slaughtered at the fiesta of Toxcatl!"

The Siege of Tenochtitlan

Now the Spaniards began to wage war against us. They attacked us by land for ten days, and then their ships appeared. Twenty days later, they gathered all their ships together near Nonohualco, off the place called Mazatzintamalco. The allies from Tlaxcala and Huexotzinco set up camp on either side of the road.

Our warriors from Tlatelolco immediately leaped into their canoes and set out for Mazatzintamalco and the Nono-hualco road. But no one set out from Tenochtitlan to assist us: only the Tlatelolcas were ready when the Spaniards arrived in their ships. On the following day, the ships sailed to Xoloco.

The fighting at Xoloco and Huitzillan lasted for two days. While the battle was under way, the warriors from Tenochtit-lan began to mutiny. They said: "Where are our chiefs? They have fired scarcely a single arrow! Do they think they have fought like men?" Then they seized four of their own leaders and put them to death. The victims were two captains, Cuauh-nochtli and Cuapan, and the priests of Amantlan and Tlalocan. This was the second time that the people of Tenochtitlan killed their own leaders.

The Flight to Tlatelolco

The Spaniards set up two cannons in the middle of the road and aimed them at the city. When they fired them, one of the shots struck the Eagle Gate. The people of the city were so terrified that they began to flee to Tlatelolco. They brought their idol Huitzilopochtli[5] with them, setting it up in the House of the Young Men. Their king Cuauhtemoc also abandoned Tenochtitlan. Their chiefs said: "Mexicanos! Tlatelolcas! All is not lost! We can still defend our houses. We can prevent them from capturing our storehouses and the produce of our lands. We can save the sustenance of life, our stores of corn. We can also save our weapons and insignia, our clusters of rich feathers, our gold earrings and precious stones. Do not be discouraged; do not lose heart. We are Mexicanos! We are Tlatelolcas!"

During the whole time we were fighting, the warriors of Tenochtitlan were nowhere to be seen. The battles at Yacacolco, Atezcapan, Coatlan, Nonohualco, Xoxohuitlan, Tepeyacac and elsewhere were all fought by ourselves, by Tlatelolcas. In the same way, the canals were defended solely by Tlatelolcas.

The captains from Tenochtitlan cut their hair short, and so did those of lesser rank. The Otomies and the other ranks that usually wore headdresses did not wear them during all the time we were fighting. The Tlatelolcas surrounded the most important captains and their women taunted them: "Why are you hanging back? Have you no shame? No woman will ever paint her face for you again!" The wives of the men from Tenochtitlan wept and begged for pity.

When the warriors of Tlatelolco heard what was happening, they began to shout, but still the brave captains of

Tenochtitlan hung back. As for the Tlatelolcas, their humblest warriors died fighting as bravely as their captains.

The Tlatelolcas Are Invited to Make a Treaty

A Spaniard named Castaneda approached us in Yauhtenco. He was accompanied by a group of Tlaxcaltecas, who shouted at the guards on the watchtower near the breakwater. These guards were Itzpalanqui, the captain of Chapultepec; two captains from Tlapala; and Cuexacaltzin. Castaneda shouted to them: "Come here!"

"What do you want?" they asked him. "We will come closer." They got into a boat and approached to within speaking distance. "Now, what have you to say to us?"

The Tlaxcaltecas asked: "Where are you from?" And when they learned that the guards were from Tlatelolco, they said: "Good, you are the men we are looking for. Come with us. The 'god' has sent for you."

The guards went with Castaneda to Nonohualco. The Captain was in the House of the Mist there, along with La Malinche, The Sun (Alvarado) and Sandoval. A number of the native lords were also present and they told the Captain: "The Tlatelolcas have arrived. We sent for them to come here."

La Malinche said to the guards: "Come forward! The Captain wants to know: what can the chiefs of Tenochtitlan be thinking of? Is Cuauhtemoc a stupid, willful little boy? Has he no mercy on the women and children of his city? Must even the old men perish? See, the kings of Tlaxcala, Huexotzinco, Cholula, Chalco, Acolhuacan, Cuauhnahuac, Xochimilco, Mizquic, Cuitlahuac and Culhuacan are all here with me."

One of the kings said: "Do the people of Tenochtitlan think they are playing a game? Already their hearts are grieving for the city in which they were born. If they will not surrender, we should abandon them and let them perish by themselves. Why should the Tlatelolcas feel sorry when the people of Tenochtitlan bring a senseless destruction on themselves?"

The guards from Tlatelolco said: "Our lords, it may be as you say."

The "god" said: "Tell Cuauhtemoc that the other kings have all abandoned him. I will go to Teocalhueyacan, where his forces are gathered, and I will send the ships to Coyoacan."

The guards returned to speak with the followers of Cuauhtemoc. They shouted the message to them from their boats. But the Tlatelolcas would not abandon the people of Tenochtitlan.

The Fighting Is Renewed

The Spaniards made ready to attack us, and the war broke out again. They assembled their forces in Cuepopan and Cozcacuahco. A vast number of our warriors were killed by their metal darts. Their ships sailed to Texopan, and the battle there lasted three days. When they had forced us to retreat, they entered the Sacred Patio, where there was a four-day battle. Then they reached Yacacolco.

The Tlatelolcas set up three racks of heads in three different places. The first rack was in the Sacred Patio of Tlilancalco [Black House], where we strung up the heads of our lords the Spaniards. The second was in Acacolco, where we strung up Spanish heads and the heads of two of their horses.

The third was in Zacatla, in front of the temple of the earth-goddess Cihuacoatl, where we strung up the heads of Tlaxcaltecas.

The women of Tlatelolco joined in the fighting. They struck at the enemy and shot arrows at them; they tucked up their skirts and dressed in the regalia of war.

The Spaniards forced us to retreat. Then they occupied the market place. The Tlatelolcas—the Jaguar Knights, the Eagle Knights, the great warriors—were defeated, and this was the end of the battle. It had lasted five days, and two thousand Tlatelolcas were killed in action. During the battle, the Spaniards set up a canopy for the Captain in the market place. They also mounted a catapult on the temple platform.

Epic Description of the Besieged City

And all these misfortunes befell us. We saw them and wondered at them; we suffered this unhappy fate.

> Broken spears lie in the roads;
> we have torn our hair in our grief.
> The houses are roofless now, and their walls
> are red with blood.
>
> Worms are swarming in the streets and plazas,
> and the walls are splattered with gore.
> The water has turned red, as if it were dyed,
> and when we drink it,
> it has the taste of brine.
>
> We have pounded our hands in despair
> against the adobe walls,

one hundred and thirty-seven

for our inheritance, our city, is lost and dead.
The shields of our warriors were its defense,
but they could not save it.

We have chewed dry twigs and salt grasses;
we have filled our mouths with dust and bits of adobe;
we have eaten lizards, rats and worms. . . .

When we had meat, we ate it almost raw. It was scarcely on the fire before we snatched it and gobbled it down.

They set a price on all of us: on the young men, the priests, the boys and girls. The price of a poor man was only two handfuls of corn, or ten cakes made from mosses or twenty cakes of salty couch-grass. Gold, jade, rich cloths, quetzal feathers—everything that once was precious was now considered worthless.

The captains delivered several prisoners of war to Cuauhtemoc to be sacrificed. He performed the sacrifices in person, cutting them open with a stone knife.

The Message from Cortes

Soon after this, the Spaniards brought Xochitl the Acolnahuacatl,[6] whose house was in Tenochtitlan, to the market place in Tlatelolco. They gripped him by both arms as they brought him there. They kept him with them for twenty days and then let him go. They also brought in a cannon, which they set up in the place where incense was sold.

The Tlatelolcas ran forward to surround Xochitl. They were led by the captain from Huitznahuac, who was a Huasteco.[7] Xochitl was placed under guard in the Temple of the Woman[8] in Axocotzinco.

one hundred and thirty-eight

As soon as the Spaniards had set Xochitl loose in the market place, they stopped attacking us. There was no more fighting, and no prisoners were taken.

Three of the great chiefs said to Cuauhtemoc: "Our prince, the Spaniards have sent us one of the magistrates, Xochitl the Acolnahuacatl. It is said that he has a message for you."

Cuauhtemoc asked them: "What is your advice?"

The chiefs all began to shout at once: "Let the message be brought here! We have made auguries with paper and with incense! The captain who seized Xochitl should bring us the message!"

The captain was sent to question Xochitl in the Temple of the Woman. Xochitl said: "The 'god' and La Malinche send word to Cuauhtemoc and the other princes that there is no hope for them. Have they no pity on the little children, the old men, the old women? What more can they do? Everything is settled.

"You are to deliver women with light skins, corn, chickens, eggs and tortillas. This is your last chance. The people of Tenochtitlan must choose whether to surrender or be destroyed."

The captain reported this message to Cuauhtemoc and the lords of Tlatelolco. The lords deliberated among themselves: "What do you think about this? What are we to do?"

The City Falls

Cuauhtemoc said to the fortune tellers: "Please come forward. What do you see in your books?"

One of the priests replied: "My prince, hear the truth

that we tell you. In only four days we shall have completed the period of eighty days. It may be the will of Huitzilopochtli that nothing further shall happen to us. Let us wait until these four days have passed."

But then the fighting broke out again. The captain of Huitznahuac—the same Huasteco who had brought in Xochitl —renewed the struggle. The enemy forced us to retreat to Amaxac. When they also attacked us there, the general flight began. The lake was full of people, and the roads leading to the mainland were all crowded.

Thus the people of Tenochtitlan and Tlatelolco gave up the struggle and abandoned the city. We all gathered in Amaxac. We had no shields and no *macanas*, we had nothing to eat and no shelter. And it rained all night.

The People Flee the City

Cuauhtemoc was taken to Cortes along with three other princes. The Captain was accompanied by Pedro de Alvarado and La Malinche.

When the princes were made captives, the people began to leave, searching for a place to stay. Everyone was in tatters, and the women's thighs were almost naked. The Christians searched all the refugees. They even opened the women's skirts and blouses and felt everywhere: their ears, their breasts, their hair. Our people scattered in all directions. They went to neighboring villages and huddled in corners in the houses of strangers.

The city was conquered in the year 3-House. The date on which we departed was the day 1-Serpent in the ninth month.[9]

The lords of Tlatelolco went to Cuauhtitlan. Even the greatest captains and warriors left in tatters. The women had only old rags to cover their heads, and they had patched together their blouses out of many-colored scraps. The chiefs were grief-stricken and mourned to one another: "We have been defeated a second time!"[10]

The Offering of Gold

A poor man was treacherously killed in Otontlan as he was seeking refuge. The other refugees were shaken by his death and began to discuss what they could do.[11] They said: "Let us beg mercy of our lord the Captain."

First the leaders of Tlatelolco demanded gold objects from everyone. They collected many lip rings, lip plugs, nose plugs and other ornaments. They searched anyone who might be hiding objects of gold behind his shield or under his clothing.

When they had gathered everything they could find, they sent the treasure to Coyoacan in the custody of several chiefs. The chiefs said to the Captain: "Our lord and master, please hear us. Your vassals, the great lords of Tlatelolco, beg you to have mercy. Your vassals and their people are being mistreated by the inhabitants of the villages where they have taken refuge. They scorn us and treacherously kill us.

"We have brought you these objects of gold, and we beg you to hear our pleas."

Then they set the baskets of gold objects before him.

When the Captain and La Malinche saw the gold, they grew very angry and said: "Is this what you have been wasting your time on? You should have been looking for the treasure that fell into the Canal of the Toltecs! Where is it? We must have it!"

The chiefs said: "Cuauhtemoc gave it to the Cihuacoatl and the Huiznahuacatl. They know where it is. Ask them."

When the Captain heard this, he ordered that the chiefs be placed in chains. La Malinche came to them later and said: "The Captain says that you may leave and speak with your leaders. He is very grateful to you. It may be true that your people are being mistreated. Tell them to return. Tell your people to come back to their houses in Tlatelolco. The Captain wants all the Tlatelolcas to reoccupy their quarter of the city. But tell your leaders that no one is to settle in Tenochtitlan itself, for that is the property of the 'gods.' You may leave now."

Cuauhtemoc Is Tortured

When the envoys from Tlatelolco had departed, the leaders of Tenochtitlan were brought before the Captain, who wished to make them talk. This was when Cuauhtemoc's feet were burned. They brought him in at daybreak and tied him to a stake.

They found the gold in Cuitlahuactonco, in the house of a chief named Itzpotonqui. As soon as they had seized it, they brought our princes—all of them bound—to Coyoacan.

About this same time, the priest in charge of the temple of Huitzilopochtli was put to death. The Spaniards had tried to learn from him where the god's finery and that of the high priests was kept. Later they were informed that it was being guarded by certain chiefs in Cuauhchichilco and Xaltocan.

Incidents After the Surrender of the Aztecs
(Proceso de Alvarado)

one hundred and forty-three

They seized it and then hanged two of the chiefs in the middle of the Mazatlan road.

The Return to Tlatelolco

The common people began to return to their houses in Tlatelolco. This was in the year 4-Rabbit. Then Temilotzin and Don Juan Huehuetzin came back, but Coyohuehuetzin and Tepantemoctzin both died in Cuaúhtitlan.

We were left entirely alone when we reoccupied Tlatelolco. Our masters, the Spaniards, did not seize any of our houses. They remained in Coyoacan and let us live in peace.

They hanged Macuilxochitl, the king of Huitzilopochco, in Coyoacan. They also hanged Pizotzin, the king of Culhuacan. And they fed the Keeper of the Black House,[12] along with several others, to their dogs.

And three wise men of Ehecatl,[13] from Tezcoco, were devoured by the dogs. They had come only to surrender; no one brought them or sent them there. They arrived bearing their painted sheets of paper. There were four of them, and only one escaped; the other three were overtaken, there in Coyoacan.

[1] The Cuetlaxteca were the allied people from Cuetlaxtla in central Mexico.
[2] Gold and silver.
[3] The fourteenth month, October 20–November 8.
[4] Present-day Cuernavaca.
[5] Not the seed-paste figure described in Chapter 9, but the wooden sculpture in the temple on top of the main pyramid.
[6] The Acolmahuacatl was a high priest from the Acolnahuac quarter inside Mexico-Tenochtitlan.
[7] An Indian from eastern Mexico.
[8] The earth-goddess Cihuacoatl.
[9] July 12–July 31.
[10] The first time by Tenochtitlan.
[11] To avoid the same fate. They wanted to return home.
[12] See Chapter 1, note 5.
[13] God of the wind, a frequent disguise of Quetzalcoatl.

Chapter Fifteen

Elegies on the Fall of the City

Introduction

By way of conclusion, we present three "songs of sorrow," true elegies written by the post-Conquest Aztec poets. The first song, from the collection of *Cantares mexicanos* in the National Library of Mexico, was probably composed in 1523. The second is part of a whole series of poems recounting the Conquest from the arrival of the Spaniards in Tenochtitlan to the ultimate defeat of the Aztecs. We have selected only the most dramatic moments from the last section of this series. The third song, also from the *Cantares mexicanos*, recalls the traditional symbolism of "flowers and songs." It laments that only grief and suffering remain in the once proud capital.

These elegies are among the first and most poignant expressions of what Dr. Garibay has called "the trauma of the Conquest." They reveal, with greater eloquence than the other texts, the deep emotional wound inflicted on the Indians by the defeat.

The Fall of Tenochtitlan

Our cries of grief rise up
and our tears rain down,
for Tlatelolco is lost.
The Aztecs are fleeing across the lake;
they are running away like women.

How can we save our homes, my people?
The Aztecs are deserting the city:
the city is in flames, and all
is darkness and destruction.

Motelchiuhtzin the Huiznahuacatl,
Tlacotzin the Tlailotlacatl,
Oquitzin the Tlacatecuhtli
are greeted with tears.

Weep, my people:
know that with these disasters
we have lost the Mexican nation.
The water has turned bitter,
our food is bitter!
These are the acts of the Giver of Life. . . .

Misfortunes of the Conquered (Archives of the Indies)

one hundred and forty-seven

The Imprisonment of Cuauhtemoc

The Aztecs are besieged in the city;
the Tlatelolcas are besieged in the city!

The walls are black,
the air is black with smoke,
the guns flash in the darkness.
They have captured Cuauhtemoc;
they have captured the princes of Mexico.

The Aztecs are besieged in the city;
the Tlatelolcas are besieged in the city!

After nine days, they were taken to Coyoacan:
Cuauhtemoc, Coanacoch, Tetlepanquetzaltzin.
The kings are prisoners now.

Tlacotzin consoled them:
"Oh my nephews, take heart!
The kings are prisoners now;
they are bound with chains."

The king Cuauhtemoc replied:
"Oh my nephew, you are a prisoner;
they have bound you in irons.

"But who is that at the side of the Captain-General?
Ah, it is Dona Isabel, my little niece!
Ah, it is true: the kings are prisoners now!

"You will be a slave and belong to another:
the collar will be fashioned in Coyoacan,
where the quetzal feathers will be woven.

"Who is that at the side of the Captain-General?
Ah, it is Dona Isabel, my little niece!
Ah, it is true: the kings are prisoners now!"

Flowers and Songs of Sorrow

Nothing but flowers and songs of sorrow
are left in Mexico and Tlatelolco,
where once we saw warriors and wise men.

We know it is true
that we must perish,
for we are mortal men.
You, the Giver of Life,
you have ordained it.

We wander here and there
in our desolate poverty.
We are mortal men.
We have seen bloodshed and pain
where once we saw beauty and valor.

We are crushed to the ground;
we lie in ruins.
There is nothing but grief and suffering
in Mexico and Tlatelolco,
where once we saw beauty and valor.

Have you grown weary of your servants?
Are you angry with your servants,
O Giver of Life?

one hundred and forty-nine

Chapter Sixteen

Aftermath

Introduction

Broken spears lay in the road, temples, and palaces; the great market, schools, and houses were in ruins; rulers, priests, sages, warriors, the youth, and the gods themselves were lost or dead. The bad omens that Motecuhzoma and others contemplated had been fulfilled: The Aztec nation appeared crushed to the ground. But was everything truly lost? The testimonies included here demonstrate the extent to which some surviving native priests and sages managed to rescue images of the tragedy that had taken place and the heroism that had sustained their people. In their annals, those with detailed pictures and glyphs and those employing the letters newly adapted by the friars to represent the sounds of their language, they recalled the ominous events, the appearance of the unexpected invaders, the acts of bravery, the devastation.

With the passing of time, while most of the ancient sacred books had been reduced to ashes, the elders and their sons, grandsons, and great-grandsons kept producing numerous manuscripts that told of their daily and difficult coexistence with the men of Castile. Documents of many different genres were composed reflecting life in these new circumstances, including many petitions asking for justice, several chronicles made up of compilations of oral traditions, numerous songs, poems, and theatrical pieces to be acted and sung, as well as translations or reworked versions of works originally in Spanish or Latin. All of these form part of an unexpectedly rich literature, which at times mixes the indigenous traditions with the content and style of what was introduced by the Europeans. As could be expected, a recurrent theme at the time, which continues to be addressed today in some works produced by contemporary Nahuas, was the tale of daily suffering and incessant confrontation. In these compositions new images of the Nahuas themselves and of the intruders are offered.

The Nahuatl language, spoken since at least the fourth century by some of the inhabitants of the metropolis of Teotihuacan, has conveyed the Aztec accounts of the Spanish conquest along with many other testimonies about the pre-Columbian, colonial, and contemporary periods. In the manner of a testimonial to the "aftermath" following the decades of conquest, I present in this chapter several particularly eloquent texts originally recorded in Nahuatl during these last two periods, including two composed only a few years ago. Together they draw vivid images of the difficult relations that have always existed between the descendants of the Aztecs and their "others"—the colonial Spaniards and contemporary Mexicans.

one hundred and fifty-one

Nahua Men of Noble Lineage
Write to the King, May 11, 1556

Only thirty-five years after the Spaniards had captured the city of Mexico-Tenochtitlan a significant number of Nahuas, mainly Aztecs, had not only learned to read and write in their language and in Spanish, but had also become acquainted with the nature of the newly imposed procedures for the presentation of claims and the filing of complaints. In particular, many of the surviving members of the native nobility and their descendants, raised in the schools of the friars, had come to develop these and other pragmatic skills. And while some of them, to preserve their privileges, collaborated with the new lords, others kept to their people and acted on their behalf.

A son of Motecuhzoma named Pedro Tlacahuepantzin and the native governors and judges of the important towns of Tlacopan (Tacuba), Iztapalapa, and Coyoacan assembled early in May 1556 to write to the king denouncing the many offenses by which they and their peoples were victimized. Dramatically describing in Nahuatl their situation, they provide a triple image of the others: of the Spaniards with whom they had to coexist, of the distant king who although unknown was thought to be good and just to his vassals, and of a Dominican friar, Bartolomé de las Casas, whom they recognized as a man "of good will and very Christian." Theirs is a powerful letter of petition.

To His Majesty [Don Philip, king of Spain], from the lords and principals [leaders] of the peoples of New Spain, May 11, 1556. . . .

Our very High and very Powerful King and Lord:

The lords and principals of the peoples of this New Spain, of Mexico and its surroundings, subjects and servants of Your Majesty, we kiss the royal feet of Your Majesty and with

one hundred and fifty-two

dutiful humility and respect we implore You and state that, given that we are in such great need of the protection and aid of Your Majesty, both for ourselves and for those whom we have in our charge, due to the many wrongs and damages that we receive from the Spaniards, because they are amongst us, and we amongst them, and because for the remedy of our necessities we are very much in need of a person who would be our defender, who would reside continuously in that royal court, to whom we could go with [our necessities], and give Your Majesty notice and true accounts of all of them, because we cannot, given the long distance there is from here to there, nor can we manifest them in writing, because they are so many and so great that it would be a great bother to Your Majesty, thus we ask and humbly beseech Your Majesty to appoint to us the bishop of Chiapas Don Fray Bartolomé de las Casas to take this charge of being our defender and that Your Majesty order him to accept; and if by chance said bishop were unable because of his death or sickness, we beseech Your Majesty in such a case to appoint to us one of the principal persons of your royal court of good will and very Christian to whom we can appeal with the things that would come up, because so many of them are of such a type that they require solely your royal presence, and from it only, after God, do we expect the remedy, because otherwise we will suffer daily so many needs and we are so aggrieved that soon we will be ended, since every day we are more consumed and finished, because they expel us from our lands and deprive us of our goods, beyond the many other labors and personal tributes that daily are increased for us.

May our Lord cause to prosper and keep the royal person and state of Our Majesty as we your subjects and servants desire. From this town of Tlacopan, where we are all assem-

one hundred and fifty-three

bled for this, the eleventh day of the month of May, the year one thousand five hundred fifty-six.

The loyal subjects and servants of your Royal Majesty, Don Esteban de Guzmán, judge of Mexico. Don Hernando Pimentel. Don Antonio Cortés. Don Juan of Coyoacan. Don Pedro de Moctezuma. Don Alonso of Iztapalapa. . . . [1]

Letter of the Council of Huejotzingo to King Philip II, 1560

The following document is a relevant section from another letter petitioning the king, this time to reduce the amount of tribute that had recently been assessed by colonial officials. The authors were members of the council of Huejotzingo (Huexotzinco), a community southeast of Mexico City that before the arrival of the Spaniards had fought with the Tlaxcalans against the "Triple Alliance" (Tenochtitlan, Tezcoco, and Tlacopan [Tacuba]). This was a region that included important poet-rulers who seemed to oppose the militarism of their more powerful neighbors.[2] This sentiment appears to continue in this text, which underlines with extraordinary detail the ethnic complexity of central Mexico as the Tlaxcalans, former and still ongoing enemies, are attacked not for being traitors, but for being unfaithful allies of the Spaniards. In Classical Nahuatl written in the elegant style of the nobility, the authors describe in vivid prose the painful aftermath following the fall of Tenochtitlan, the variety of responses to Christianity at that time, and the great esteem in which they and others held the conqueror of the Aztec city.

Our Lord sovereign, you the king don Felipe. . . .

[B]efore anyone told us of or made us acquainted with your fame and your story, . . . and before we were told or taught the glory and name of our Lord God, . . . when your servants the Spaniards reached us and your captain general don Hernando Cortés arrived, . . . our Lord God the ruler of heaven and possessor of earth . . . enlightened us so that we took you as our king to belong to you and become your people and your subjects; not a single town surpassed us here in New Spain in that first and earliest we threw ourselves toward you, we gave ourselves to you, and furthermore no one intimidated us, no one forced us into it, but truly God caused us to deserve that voluntarily we adhered to you so that we gladly received the newly arrived Spaniards who reached us here in New Spain. . . . We received them very gladly, we embraced them, we saluted them with many tears, though we were not acquainted with them, and our fathers and grandfathers also did not know them; but by the mercy of our Lord God we truly came to know them. Since they are our neighbors, therefore we loved them; nowhere did we attack them. Truly we fed them and served them; some arrived sick, so that we carried them in our arms and on our backs, and we served them in many other ways which we are not able to say here. Although the people who are called and named Tlaxcalans indeed helped, yet we strongly pressed them to give aid, and we admonished them not to make war; but though we so admonished them, they made war and fought for fifteen days. But we, when a Spaniard was afflicted, without fail at once we managed to reach him. . . . We do not lie in this, for all the conquerors know it well, those who have died and some now living.

And when they began their conquest and war-making, then also we prepared ourselves well to aid them, for out came all of our war gear, our arms and provisions and all our equipment, and we not merely named someone, we went in person, we who rule, and we brought all our nobles and all of our vassals to aid the Spaniards. We helped not only in warfare, but we also gave them everything they needed; we fed and clothed them, and we would carry in our arms and on our backs those whom they wounded in war or who were very ill, and we did all the tasks in preparing for war. And so that they could fight the Mexica with boats, we worked hard; we gave them the wood and pitch with which the Spaniards made the boats. And when they conquered the Mexica and all belonging to them, we never abandoned them or left them behind in it. And when they went to conquer Michoacan, Jalisco, and Colhuacan, and there at Pánuco and there at Oaxaca and Tehuantepec and Guatemala, [we were] the only ones who went along while they conquered and made war here in New Spain until they finished the conquest; we never abandoned them, in no way did we prejudice their war-making, though some of us were destroyed in it [there was no one as deserving as we], for we did our duty very well. But as to those Tlaxcalans, several of their nobles were hanged for making war poorly; in many places they ran away, and often did badly in the war. In this we do not lie, for the conquerors know it well.

Our lord sovereign, we also say and declare before you that your fathers the twelve sons of St. Francis reached us, whom the very high priestly ruler the Holy Father sent and whom you sent, both taking pity on us so that they came to teach us the gospel, to teach us the holy Catholic faith and belief, to make us acquainted with the single deity God our Lord, and likewise God favored us and enlightened us, us of Huejotzingo, who dwell in your city, so that we gladly received them. When they entered the city of Huejotzingo, of our own free will we honored them and showed them esteem. When they embraced us so that we would abandon the wicked belief in many gods, we forthwith voluntarily left it; likewise they did us the good deed [of telling us] to destroy and burn the stones and wood that we worshiped as gods, and we did it; very willingly we destroyed, demolished, and burned the temples. Also when they gave us the holy gospel, the holy Catholic faith, with very good will and desire we received and grasped it; no one frightened us into it, no one forced us, but very willingly we seized it, and they gave us all the sacraments. Quietly and peacefully we arranged and ordered it among ourselves; no one, neither nobleman nor commoner, was ever tortured or burned for this, as was done on every hand here in New Spain. [The people of] many towns were forced and tortured, were hanged or burned, because they did not want to leave idolatry, and unwillingly they received the gospel and faith. Especially those Tlaxcalans pushed out and rejected the fathers, and would not receive the faith, for many of the high nobles were burned, and some hanged, for combating the advocacy and service of our Lord God. But we of Huejotzingo, we your poor vassals, we never did anything in your harm, always we served you in every command you sent or what at your command we were ordered. . . . Therefore now, in and through God, may you hear these our words, . . . so that you will exercise on us your rulership to console us and aid us in [this trouble] with which daily we weep and are sad. We are afflicted and sore pressed, and your town and city of Huejotzingo is as if it is about to disappear and be destroyed. Here is what is being done to us: now your stewards the royal officials and the prosecuting attorney Dr. Maldonado are assessing us a very great tribute to belong to you. The tribute we are to give is 14,800 pesos in money, and also all the bushels of maize.

one hundred and fifty-seven

Our lord sovereign, never has such happened to us in all the time since your servants and vassals the Spaniards came to us, for your servant don Hernando Cortés, late captain general, the Marqués del Valle, in all the time he lived here with us, always greatly cherished us and kept us happy; he never disturbed nor agitated us. Although we gave him tribute, he assigned it to us only with moderation; even though we gave him gold, it was only very little; no matter how much, no matter in what way, or if not very pure, he just received it gladly. He never reprimanded us or afflicted us, because it was evident to him and he understood well how very greatly we served and aided him. Also he told us many times that he would speak in our favor before you, that he would help us and inform you of all the ways in which we have aided and served you. . . . But perhaps before you he forgot us. How then shall we speak? We did not reach you, we were not given audience before you. Who then will speak for us? Unfortunate are we. Therefore now we place ourselves before you, our sovereign lord. . . .

Your poor vassals who bow down humbly to you from afar,

Don Leonardo Ramírez, governor. Don Mateo de la Corona, alcalde. . . . Toribio de San [Cristó]bal Motolinía.[3]

An Eighteenth-Century Nahua Testimony

(Introduced as if it were a text from 1531)

The vanquished communities became involved in innumerable litigations to defend themselves and their lands. The General

Archives of the Nation in Mexico City, along with others throughout the country, preserve thousands of documents in Nahuatl produced during the lawsuits, some of which include native drawings and glyphs. In the following example from this legal genre one can make out the language of bitter protest and resignation of the people of Santo Tomás Ajusco, a community in the southern part of the Federal District that encompasses Mexico City. The words, attributed to a native leader said to have founded the town in 1531, were presented to the Spanish authorities in 1710 by the community's inhabitants. Through the invented narrative the descendants of the Aztecs sought to support their rights to the town's adjacent lands. The aim was to present the text as a copy of a lost original while contending that its testimony represented speech uttered almost two hundred years before.

From internal evidence this text can be related to the several manuscripts known as Techialoyan codices, which made their appearance early in the eighteenth century as copies of or supplements to the much required but by then lost pre-Hispanic communal land titles. To the extent that this text is of the same type, the Ajusco testimony has a double significance: as a Nahuatl document used in litigation and as an eighteenth-century representation of the sorrowful expressions the Nahuatl ancestors *should* have pronounced when, as refugees, they established themselves on the slopes of the Ajusco mountain. The text asserts that in 1531 their chief had taken possession of their communal lands.

My beloved children, today on the second day of *Toxcatl* [one of the 20-days "months"] of 1531, on the day that belongs to the one . . . true God, who is in heaven and on the earth and everywhere in the world; . . . know that everywhere the lords who are in charge of the people are very sad because of what . . . the white men of Castile have done and are still doing. . . .

one hundred and fifty-nine

It is obvious how they punish the revered lords of the towns, those who were in charge of the people, who had the rod [symbol of authority]; it is clear how they are put in prison, because the men of Castile are not satisfied with what they are given, and [they] do not surrender their gold nor their precious stones.

It is well known how they jeer at our revered women and daughters. They are not quiet, except solely with gold and precious stones. They make fun of the wives of those who ruled. They are not quiet but when they burn the others, as they burned alive the greatly revered lord of Michoacan, the great Caltzontzin. Thus they behaved with other great lords who were in charge, who ruled there in Xalapan, Tlaxcalan, Tecuantepec, Oaxyacac, and [other] towns and chiefdoms where the envious, gold-hungry Christians also entered. . . . How much blood was shed! It was our fathers' blood! And what for? Why was it done? Learn it once and for all: because they want to impose themselves upon us, because they are utterly gold hungry, voracious of what belongs to others: our chiefdoms, our revered women and daughters, and our lands.

It is known that the Castilian Cortés, the recently named Marqués del Valle, was authorized, there in Castile, to come to distribute our lands. Thus it is said . . . that secretly the lord Marqués will come to take our lands, take possession of ourselves and establish new towns. And where will they throw us? Where will they place us? A very great sadness afflicts us. What will we do, my sons?

Still my heart recovers. I [i.e., the supposed founder of the city] remember, I will establish a town here . . . on the slopes of Axochco mountain, in Xaltipac [On the Sand's Surface]. Because from down there to here is the place of the men of Axochco. From down there on, this land is ours, it was left to us by our grandfathers, it was their property since ancient times.

I remember, I will establish a little temple where we will place the new god that the men from Castile have given us. Truly this new god wants us to worship him. What will we do, my sons? Let us receive the water on our heads [be baptized], let us give ourselves to the men of Castile, perhaps in this way they will not kill us.

Let us remain here. Do not trespass [by] going on another's land, perhaps in this way they will not kill us. Let us follow them; thus, perhaps we will awaken their compassion. It will be good if we surrender entirely to them. Oh, that the true god who resides in heaven will help us [coexist] close to the men of Castile.

And in order that they will not kill us, we will not claim all our lands. We will reduce in length the extension of our lands, and that which remains, our fathers will defend.

Now I declare that, in order for them not to kill us, . . . we accept to have water poured on our heads, that we worship the new god, as I declare he is the same as the one we had.

Now I reduce in length our lands. Thus it will be. Their limits will begin in the direction from which the sun rises and continue . . . [he mentions each of the limits].

I presume that for this small piece of land they will not kill us. It does not matter that it was much larger. This is my decision because I do not want my sons to be killed. Therefore, we will work only this little piece of land, and thus our sons will do so. Let us hope in this manner they will not kill us. . . .[4]

Dance of the Great Conquest, Eighteenth Century

In many different forms Nahuatl-speaking people continued over the centuries to express their feelings about what had befallen them. Among the extant testimonies that recall the Spanish invasion, there are several compositions conceived to be performed accompanied by music, song, and dance. They are productions belonging to a genre of native plays that were developed throughout the colonial period. Among the numerous "dances" or ballet-dramas whose theme is the "Conquest," there is one written in elegant Nahuatl that deserves special consideration, among other reasons because it was still being performed as late as 1894 in the town of Xicotepec (today Villa Juárez) in the state of Puebla.

As is common in Greek drama, the plot of the "Dance of the Great Conquest" develops in a single day. The story concerns the arrival of Hernan Cortés, his encounter with Motecuhzoma, and some important events said to have immediately followed the meeting. The text conveys a type of Christian lesson centered on the benefits believed to have come from Cortés's advent as the bearer of the true faith. From this one can infer the intervention of a friar's hand; yet at the same time it includes a dialogue between Motecuhzoma and prince Cuauhtemoc that no one but a Nahua could have introduced. This dialogue transforms the play, perhaps created originally as a piece of "missionary theater," into a courageous condemnation both of the Spanish intrusion and of Motecuhzoma's attitude toward Cortés, which we discussed earlier in chapter 4. This attack, uttered by Cuauhtemoc, is accompanied by a contemptuous depiction of the conqueror and his men.

The fact that this play, whose language is indicative of an eighteenth-century composition, was performed as recently as 1894 demonstrates the enduring force of the collective memory of the Nahuas, which could keep alive sentiments associated with an event that, although it had radically affected their culture and being, occurred in a distant past. Numerous anachronisms and fanciful interpretations of historical facts are understandably present throughout the play. For example, Cuauhtemoc refers to Motecuhzoma as "the great ruler who governs this new land called America." And due most likely to the friar's intervention, following Cuauhtemoc's reprimand of Motecuhzoma the play ends with an imaginary mortal combat in which Cuauhtemoc loses his life. This fight, which supposedly took place on the same day, deviates widely from the accepted historical facts, which identify the Aztec leader's death as taking place when he was hanged by Cortés in Tabasco in 1525. In the spirit of a sermon, a choir sings: "There died poor Cuauhtemoc. He went to Hell. Because of his blindness, his perdition took place."

This admonition, made to be enunciated in an edifying manner, contrasts with the young prince's courageous rebuke against Motecuhzoma. The words, notwithstanding a few anachronisms, ring true to our understanding of the character of the last Aztec "emperor."

Emperor Motecuhzoma, great Lord, Monarch, as you are named here in the land called America.

Improperly are you so named, for you no longer ought to wear the crown, for you have lost courage and you are afraid. . . . Tell me if you dare to speak to this great city? Can you give [something] to those who are down and out in the country from which they came?

They come to mock you. All those who come here are second rate or Spaniards who lost out, who come telling you that in their country there are great cities, talking of another king at the head of the empire of Castile by the name of Charles the Fifth, [and] of a Catholic religion.

These are only stories, lies. I do not believe in other books [i.e., except indigenous, picto-glyphic codices]. I feel that their words are only like dreams. You have no courage, but I have, and I will make war and test the strength they claim to have. I shall see it, and many fearful arts will be practiced. There are flints, arrows, new stones. Flints that they will take, those who go out to war, fearful warriors, also Chichimecs, like wild beasts who maintain their anger. They are making straight [truthful] my gods, they all give me great knowledge, science. I shall lead them. I shall encourage them, all who come together, and they [the] armies will show every form of war.

You will likewise lose your kingdom, your crown, and your scepter. You will lose all the esteem that I maintained for you because you gave yourself up. I will search for you in your . . . kingdom, and you shall suffer those lost ones here present, the bandits, Spaniards who have come over here. They come to fool you, for you no longer deserve your dominion.

I deserve it. It belongs to me because I am strong of heart, valiant. I do not want the honor of our gods to come to nothing. You shall see, you shall experience who is the one who calls himself, who is named prince Cuauhtemoc. I have in my hands flames, noise, lightning, embers, smoke, sand, dust, winds, whirlwinds with which I shall drive them back. If they do not want to die, let them go right back to their country. If they do not, they shall perish here no matter what you do to prevent it.[5]

The Manifestos of Emiliano Zapata, April 1918

Nahuatl-speaking Indians and other natives, among them the Yaqui of Sonora and the Maya of Yucatan, took part in the Mexican Revolution of 1910–19. Emiliano Zapata, a well-known leader of the Revolution and champion of the landless peasants of southern Mexico, was not himself an Indian, but he was a mestizo, born in Anencuilco, a small town in Morelos, who, endowed with a charismatic personality, had managed to attract large numbers of Nahuas and others to join the army he had raised. However, the mere idea of an Indian uprising caused such alarm among the elite that a prominent conservative congressman, José Maria Lozano, warned his fellow partisans of Zapata's successes and threat in these terms: "Zapata has rebelled. . . . He poses as the liberator of the slave; he offers something to all. He is not alone. . . . Countless people follow him. . . . He offers them lands. His preaching begins to bear fruit: the Indians have rebelled!"[6]

Several testimonies exist that describe the pleasure felt by the Nahuas on hearing Zapata addressing them in their own language. One is provided by a native woman, Luz Jiménez, in an account she gave of Zapata's arrival in the village of Milpa Alta, just south of Mexico City: "First news we had about the revolution was the arrival of a great man, Zapata, who came from the state of Morelos. He was well dressed with his tall, crowned, broad-brimmed felt *sombrero*. He was the first great man who spoke to us in Nahuatl. . . . All those who came along with him spoke Nahuatl very much the same as we do. Zapata spoke Nahuatl! When he and his men entered Milpa Alta we could understand what they said."[7]

Emiliano Zapata, who became a legendary hero to thousands of mestizo peasants and Indians, was fighting to get back for them the communal lands that had been usurped by Spaniards, Mexicans, and others of European provenance over the course of centuries. To the eyes of his followers, Zapata's struggle was a fight to regain lost personal freedom and ancestral lands, a battle to assure that land would be owned only by those who worked it.

After several years of fighting, and already suffering from a decimated army, Zapata tried to regain his forces by issuing two manifestos in Nahuatl on April 27, 1918. In one he urged some Tlaxcalan armed bands, who had previously followed Domingo Arenas, his former ally and later his murdered rival, to come to his side. In the other he repeated the call to the people living in the nearby villages. These manifestos are the last extant examples of public documents in Nahuatl in which, once again, the images of the vanquished and of those who abuse power are vividly depicted. The first manifesto reads as follows:

To you, chiefs, officers, and soldiers of the Arenas Division.

What we all suspected has already occurred. That which had to happen today or tomorrow: your separation from those engendered by Venustiano Carranza [president and head of the federal army]. They never favored, nor loved you. They merely deceived you, envied you. They wanted to hurt you, dishonor you, get rid of you. They never behaved as humans toward you.

To turn the face against those who so badly abuse power, honors you, erases the memory of your past deception [when their chief Arenas sided with the federal government].

We hope you will take part in the ideals for which we are fighting. In this manner we will be one, pressed closely against one flag. Thus our unified hearts will excel. Those who make fun of us, the ones engendered by Carranza, will not be able to destroy us. . . .

Join us, our flag belongs to the people. We will fight together. . . . [T]his is our great work which we will achieve in some way, before our revered mother, [the one] called *Patria* [i.e., homeland or ancestral land].

one hundred and sixty-six

Let us fight the perverse, wicked Carranza, who is a tormentor of us all. If we work for our unity, we will fulfill the great command: land, liberty, justice. Let us perform our work of revolutionaries and know our duties toward our revered mother the [ancestral] land. This army's command invites you. That is why I express this word. All those who will follow it, who will fight at our side, will enjoy a righteous and good life. In it we place our word of honor, of sincere men and good revolutionaries.

Tlaltizapan, Morelos, April 27, 1918

The Commander-in-Chief of the Liberation Army, Emiliano Zapata[8]

The other manifesto, dated the same day, was addressed to the people in general who lived in the region "where chief Arenas had fought." Here Zapata expresses himself echoing the centuries-old complaints and hopes of the Nahuas:

Our great war will not come to an end, will not conclude until that obscure tyrant, envious, who mocks the people, makes their faces turn around, is defeated. He is Venustiano Carranza who dishonors and makes ashamed our revered mother the [ancestral] land, Mexico. . . .

Here is the people who keep strong and confront the great possessors of lands — Christians [i.e., hacienda owners and caiques], those who have made fun of us, who hate us. . . . We will receive the valiant ones, our hearts will rejoice being together with them. . . .

one hundred and sixty-seven

Let us keep fighting. We will not rest until we come to possess our lands, those that belonged to our grandfathers, and which the greedy-handed thieves took from us. . . .

It is now more than ever necessary that we all, with our heart and courage, achieve this great work, following those who began the uprising, who preserve in their souls the true aims and have faith in a pure life.

The Commander-in-Chief of the Liberation Army, Emiliano Zapata[9]

The Nahuas and the "Coyotes" Today

The Nahuas, their invincible spirit, and their language are still very much alive today. Contrary to what some had expected or even desired, indigenous endurance, after hundreds of years of adversity, has made possible the survival of a people with a long cultural history. Today, in the last decade of our millennium, there are more than forty million native people in the Americas, one and a half million of whom are Nahuas engaged in the centuries-long struggle to preserve and foster their ancestral cultural identities. The intellectual effort of a growing number of them is currently contributing to a renaissance that includes the production of a new literature, aptly named by them *Yancuic Tlahtolli*, the "New Word."

Among the contemporary Nahua writers we find professionals teaching in rural communities, journalists, and university students. Some are already well acquainted with Nahuatl grammar and the ancient literature inscribed in the language. To them the compositions of pre-Columbian poets, such as the famous Nezahualcoyotl (1402–1472), the extant literary narratives, and the detailed chronicles — including those concerning the Spanish invasion found in this book — are a source of inspiration. It has been a great honor and pleasure for me that some of these masters of the "new word" have attended the seminar on Nahuatl culture and language which I have conducted for more than thirty years at the National University of Mexico.

One of these native authors, Joel Martínez Hernández, born in the Huaxteca in the state of Hidalgo and himself a teacher, has penned in Nahuatl a literary declaration expressing his thoughts regarding the present and future of the Nahuas. In it he paints a painful image of those he and many Nahuas call "Coyotes," referring to the astute and voracious non-Indians who take advantage of the few possessions left to the indigenous peoples.

Some Coyotes are saying
that we Nahuas will disappear,
will vanish,
our language will be heard no more,
will be used no more.
The Coyotes rejoice in this,
as this is what they are looking for.
Why is it that they want us to disappear?
We do not have to contemplate this too long,
because four hundred years have shown us
the aim of the Coyotes.
They are envious of our lands,
our forests and rivers,
our work, our sweat.
The Coyotes want us living
in the slums of their cities,
naked and hungry,
subject to their falsehoods and frauds.
The Coyotes want us to work for them,
they want us to abandon
our communal lands, our labor,

our endeavors and language,
our ways of dressing and living,
our forms of thinking.
The Coyotes desire
to make Coyotes out of us,
and then they will deprive us
of all that is ours,
the fruits of our labor
which has caused us fatigue.
We must strengthen our hearts
with one, two words,
which will illuminate our eyes,
so we can become fully conscious of it.
We have many tasks to perform.
I will add only a few words.
Where and how many
are the Nahuas in Mexico?
We, the Nahuas,
are not just in one place,
we are scattered in sixteen states
and eight hundred and eight municipalities.
One has to understand
that it is not only in our farm[s],
not only in our village[s],
that we Nahuas exist.
Sometimes we hear
that we Nahuas are vanishing,
but the census figures
speak very differently. . . .
Truly we can assert that,
although some want us to disappear,

we Nahuas continue to live,
we Nahuas continue to grow. . . .[10]

The Nahuas, formerly vanquished and for centuries oppressed, are indeed growing in numbers and, above all, have become fully conscious of the right they have to preserve their language and culture. With this assurance, today they are busily reflecting upon their culture and its destiny. The "others," imagined and described in many forms by them since the days of the invasion, must come to grips with and understand this new perspective. As is daily becoming more evident, the Nahuas and the millions of other Native Americans throughout the hemisphere are no longer asking for mercy. Like other Americans, north and south of the equator, they know they have their rights as individuals, communities, and ethnic groups. But now another issue has come to the fore: How does one learn to trust in oneself? Some indigenous writers claim that for this to take place a new self-image must be created. One Nahua poet, Natalio Hernández Xocoyotzin, a native of Ixhuatan, Veracruz, has conveyed this insight beautifully.

Sometimes I feel
that we, the Indians, are waiting
for the arrival of a Man
who can achieve all,
    knows everything,
is ready to help us,
will answer our problems.

But, this Man
who can achieve all,
    knows everything,
will never arrive

one hundred and seventy-one

because he is in ourselves,
walks along with us.
He has been asleep,
but now he is awakening.[11]

The broken spears, the net made of holes, was it all merely a dream? Ancient poetry was like "the flowers that wither," as a fifteenth-century Nahua poet expressed it. But now it is different. The "person-within" is already awakening, giving strength to the heart of the Nahuas. The words of that inner American being are different from those heard daily in our busy lives, but by listening carefully one can perceive in them the wisdom of the Nahua elders.

They shall not wither, my flowers,
they shall not cease, my songs,
I, the singer, lift them up.
They are scattered, they spread about.
But even though my flowers may yellow,
they shall live
in the innermost house
of the bird of the golden feathers.[12]

---

[1] This letter, preserved in the General Archive of the Indies, Seville, is amply commented in "Bartolomé de las Casas in the Indigenous Consciousness of the Sixteenth Century," chap. 4, M. Leon-Portilla, *Endangered Cultures*, trans. Julie Goodson-Lawes (Dallas: Southern Methodist University Press, 1990), pp. 85–96.

[2] See M. Leon-Portilla, *The Aztec Image of Self and Society: An Introduction to Nahua Culture*, ed. J. Jorge Klor de Alva (Salt Lake City: University of Utah Press, 1992), chap. 5.

[3] This letter – Doc. 165, Archivo Histórico Nacional, Madrid – republished with permission, is found in Arthur J. O. Anderson, Frances Berdan, and James Lockhart, eds. and trans., *Beyond the Codices: The Nahua View of Colonial Mexico* (Berkeley: University of California Press, 1976), pp. 181–87.

[4] "Corporate land title of Santo Tomás Ajusco," General Archive of the Nation, Mexico City, Section "Lands" (Tierras) 2676. The Nahuatl text and an ancient Spanish version of it have been published by Marcelo Díaz de Salas and Luis Reyes García in "Testimonio de la Fundación de Santo Tomás Ajusco," *Tlalocan* (Mexico: National Autonomous University of Mexico, 1970), vol. 6, pp. 193–212.

[5] A copy of the Nahuatl text of this "dance" was recorded by the ethnologist Bodil Christensen in Xiutepec, renamed Villa Juárez, in the state of Puebla.

6 Discourse transcribed in Gildardo Magaña, *Emiliano Zapata y el agrarismo in Mexico* (Mexico: 1937), p. 30.

7 Testimony in Nahuatl of doña Luz Jiménez, included in Fernando Horcasitas, *De Porfirio Díaz a Zapata, Memoria Náhuatl de Milpa Alta* (Mexico: National Autonomous University of Mexico, 1974), p. 105.

8 "Manifiesto a los Jefes, oficiales y soldados de la Division Arenas," Archive of Zapata, preserved at the National University, Mexico, file 29.

9 "Manifiesto a los pueblos comprendidos en la zona de operaciones de la Division Arenas," Archive of Zapata, preserved at the National University of Mexico, file 29. The full text in Nahuatl of the two manifestos with an ample commentary is found in M. Leon-Portilla, *Los manifiestos en náhuatl de Emiliano Zapata* (Mexico: National Autonomous University of Mexico, 1978).

10 Joel Martínez Hernández, "¿Quesqui Nahuamacehualme Tiiztoqueh?" (How Many Nahuas Are We?), in *Nahua Macehualpaquiliztli* (Joy of the Nahua People) (Mexico: 1983), pp. 4–9.

11 Natalio Hernández Xocoyotzin, *Cempoalxochitl, veinte flores, una sola flor*, bilingual edition, Nahuatl-Spanish (Mexico: National Autonomous University of Mexico, 1987), pp. 30–31.

12 Colección de cantares mexicanos (Collection of Mexican songs), National Library of Mexico, MS 1628 bis, folio 16 v.

Appendix

The chronicles and other accounts written by the men who discovered and conquered the New World were a startling revelation to the Europe of the sixteenth and seventeenth centuries. The Old World, with its long history, was suddenly eager to learn more about the "barbarous peoples" who had recently been discovered, and the reports brought or sent back by the "chroniclers of the Indies" were received with the liveliest interest. At times these new facts were questioned or disputed, but they never failed to elicit reflection and interpretation. The conquistadors themselves attempted to describe clearly, in European terms, the different physical and human realities existing in the New World; so also did the missionary friars and the European philosophers and humanists, as well as the royal historians.

The results were varied. Some were "projections" of old ideas: for instance, Fray Diego de Duran argued that the Nahuas[1] were actually the descendants of the Lost Tribes of Israel. Others were apologies—more or less intentional—for the Conquest, such as the letter-reports of Cortes. The Indians appear in some chronicles as idolatrous savages given over to cannibalism and sodomy, while in others they are described as models of natural virtue.

On the basis of these reports and chronicles, a number of histories were written in Europe from the humanistic point of view of that epoch. One outstanding example is *De Orbe Novo* by the celebrated Pedro Martir de Angleria, who often expresses his amazement on discovering the arts and folkways of the Indians; another is the wealth of firsthand material which the royal chronicler, Antonio de Herrera, incorporated in his *Historia general de los hechos de los castellanos en las Islas y Tierra Firme de el Mar*

Oceano. European historiography—not only in Spain and Portugal, but also in France, England, Germany and Italy—gained new life when it turned its attention to the reports coming back from the New World.

We rarely consider, however, that if Europe showed so great an interest in this astonishing new continent, the Indians must have shown an equal interest in the Spaniards, who to them were strange beings from a totally unknown world. It is attractive to study the different ways in which the Europeans conceived of the Indians, but the inverse problem, which takes us to the heart of indigenous thought, is perhaps even more instructive. What did the Indians think when they saw the strangers arrive on their shores and in their cities? What were their first attitudes toward the invaders? In what spirit did they fight them? And how did they interpret their own downfall?

There are no complete and final answers to these questions; but there are some partial answers, provided by the native cultures that had then attained the highest development—the Mayas of Yucatan and the Nahuas of the Valley of Mexico. The Spanish accounts of the Conquest are only one version of it; the Indians who were its victims recorded another, in words and pictures. Inevitably there are major disagreements between the two versions. But in spite of all the mutual accusations and misunderstandings, or perhaps because of them, both accounts are intensely human. They should be studied without prejudice, for only a calm examination, free of bias and preconceptions, can help to explain the Mexican people of today, who are the living consequence of that violent clash between two worlds.

Within Middle America, the Nahuatl and Mayan cultures left us the most ample indigenous descriptions of the Conquest. Both cultures possessed a mode of writing, an oral tradition and a sense of history. A brief consideration of their efforts to record the past will illustrate their earnest desire to depict their own version of this most shattering event.

The Mayan stelae, the other commemorative monuments of the Mayas and Nahuas, and the historical codices or *xiuhamatl* (books of years) of the Nahuas all testify to the care with which both cultures chronicled the important events in their past. These records were complemented by oral texts, which were faithfully passed down by memory in the pre-Hispanic centers of education. Students were taught, among other things, the history of what had happened year by year, an amplified version of what was contained in the codices.

A single contemporary report will make clear the Indians' concern to preserve their history. It is taken from the *Historia general* by Don Antonio de Herrera, royal chronicler of Philip II. Don Antonio never pretended to glorify the Indians, but he gathered together, better than anyone else, a great mass of reports and information concerning them. In section four, book ten, he observes:

The nations of New Spain preserved the memory of their antiquities. In Yucatan and Honduras there were certain books in which the Indians recorded the events of their times, together with their knowledge of plants, animals and other natural things.

In the Province of Mexico, they had libraries of histories and calendars, which they painted in pictures. Whatever had a concrete form was painted in its own image, while if it lacked a form, they represented it by other characters. Thus they set down what they wished.

And to remember the times in which each event came to pass, they had certain wheels, each of which represented a century of a hundred and two years. Also, depending on the year in which memorable events took place, they painted their pictures and characters, such as a man wearing a helmet and a red mantle, under the sign of the canestalk, to show the year in which the Castilians entered their land, and so with the other events.

And because their characters were not sufficient, like our own writing, they could not set things down exactly, only the substance of their ideas; but they learned in chorus many speeches, orations and songs. They took great care to see that the youths learned them by memory, and for this they had schools in which the old taught them to the young. By this means, the texts were preserved in their entirety.

And when the Castilians entered that land and taught the Indians the art of writing, the natives wrote out their speeches and songs as they had known them since antiquity. They also recorded their discourses in their own characters and figures, and in this manner they set down the Paternoster, the Ave Maria and all of the Christian doctrine.

In all these ways, Nahuas and Mayas recorded the most impressive and tragic event in their history—the fall of their civilization at the hands of strangers, ending with the destruction of their ancient ways of life. The present book, a kind of anthology of texts and pictures, offers some examples of the different impressions preserved by the Nahuatl-speaking Indians regarding Cortes and the Spaniards, the events of the Conquest and the final ruin of the Aztec capital and its culture.

A similar book could be prepared on the Mayas, who also left indigenous accounts of the Conquest, including those in the *Anales de los Xahil*, the *Titulos de la Casa Ixquin-Nehaip* and the *Cronica de Chac-Xulub-Chen*, and at least fragments in certain books of the *Chilam Balam*. But this task remains for those who dedicate themselves to the study of Mayan civilization.

We must turn next to a brief discussion of the various sources from which these Nahuatl records of the Conquest have been selected.

Indian Texts and Paintings Describing the Conquest

Fray Toribio de Benavente, known as Motolinia, arrived in Tenochtitlan in June 1524, one of a celebrated group of twelve Franciscan friars. He was the first to discover the Indians' determination to preserve their own memories of the Conquest. In the beginning of the third part of his *Historia de los indios de la Nueva España*, he reported:

Among the events of their times, the native Indians took particular note of the year in which the Spaniards entered this land, for to them it was a most remarkable happening which at first caused them great terror and amazement. They saw a strange people arrive from the sea—a feat they had never before witnessed nor had known was possible—all dressed in strange garments and so bold and warlike that, although few in number, they could invade all the provinces of this land imperiously, as if the natives were their vassals. The Indians were also filled with wonder at their horses, and the Spaniards riding on their backs.... They called the Spaniards "teteuh," meaning "gods," which the Spaniards corrupted into "teules."...

The Indians also set down the year in which the twelve friars arrived together....

There are twelve surviving documents, written or painted, in which the Indians described the coming of the Spaniards and the great conflict that ensued. They are not of equal importance and antiquity, but they reveal the characteristic impressions that the Nahuas formed of the Conquest. The most valuable of these documents are:

(1) *Songs of the Conquest.* The oldest native accounts of the Conquest are in the form of songs, composed in the traditional manner by some of the few surviving *cuicapicque*, or Nahuatl poets. True *icnocuicatl* (songs of sorrow) are the stanzas describing the final days of Tenochtitlan (in Chapter 14) and the grief of the Mexican people over their defeat (in Chapter 15). As Dr. Angel Maria Garibay has pointed out in his *Historia de la literatura nahuatl*, the first of these poems must have been composed in about 1524, the second a year earlier.

(2) *Unos anales historicos de la nacion mexicana.* This title has been given to the important "Manuscript 22" in the National Library in Paris. The manuscript dates from 1528, only seven years after the fall of the Aztec capital, and was written in Nahuatl by a group of anonymous natives of Tlatelolco. The most remarkable thing about this document is the fact that its Indian authors some-

how learned the correct use of the Latin alphabet (the Colegio de Santa Cruz had not yet been founded) in order to write out some of their memories of past events—above all, their own account of the Conquest. The work is valuable to us as historical evidence, but its literary and human value is perhaps even greater. It presents for the first time, and in detail, a picture of the destruction of Nahuatl culture, as witnessed by a few of its survivors. The relevant passages from the manuscript, which has been translated from Nahuatl into Spanish by Dr. Garibay, are given in Chapter 14 of this book.

(3) *Codex Florentino.* The description of the Conquest preserved in this codex was recorded later than that in "Manuscript 22," but it is much more ample. It was written in Nahuatl, under the eye of Fray Bernadino de Sahagun, by his Indian students from Tlatelolco and elsewhere, using the reminiscences of aged natives who had actually seen the Conquest. The first version of the text—"in the Indian language, and in the crude manner in which they spoke it"—seems to have been completed in about 1555; unfortunately it has been lost. Fray Bernadino later made a resume of it in Spanish. Still later, in about 1585, he prepared a second version in Nahuatl to correct the first, which, he said, contained "certain things that were not true, and was silent about certain others where it should have spoken. . . ."

As Dr. Garibay has remarked, it is impossible to say whether the text has gained or lost from these emendations. It is, however, the most complete indigenous account of the Conquest now known —from the sighting of various omens "when the Spaniards had not yet come to this land" to a transcript of one of the speeches "in which Don Hernando Cortes admonished all the lords of Mexico, Tezcoco and Tlacopan" to deliver their gold and other treasures. We have drawn a number of selections from this invaluable source.

(4) *The major pictographic records.* The texts by Sahagun's informants and other native historians are supplemented by various records in which events of the Conquest are set down as paintings, the traditional Indian manner of writing history. The three prin-

cipal works of this nature are the paintings corresponding to the Nahuatl texts by Sahagun's informants, preserved in the *Codex Florentino;* the *Lienzo de Tlaxcala* (dating from the middle of the sixteenth century), a collection of eighty paintings describing the actions of the Tlaxcaltecas, a subject tribe who allied themselves with the Spaniards; and the improperly named *Manuscrito de 1576* (it mentions several later dates), also known as the *Codex Aubin,* with both texts and related paintings. There are also some pictures, clearly indigenous in nature, in the manuscript called the *Codex Ramirez.* This codex was probably compiled from the data assembled before 1580 by Fray Diego de Duran, who is known to have had access to many other native accounts which have since been lost.

The illustrations for the present book were adapted by Alberto Beltran from the paintings contained in these works.

(5) *Briefer indigenous accounts.* We have also drawn several passages from briefer works in Nahuatl. The *Codex Aubin* is especially valuable; one of the descriptions of the massacre at the chief temple (in Chapter 9) was taken from it. Other important material was set down by Fernando Alvarado Tezozomoc in his two chronicles, *"mexicana"* and *"mexicayotl,"* and by the celebrated historian of Chalco, Domingo Francisco de San Anton Munon Chimalpain Cuauhtlehuanitzin. From Chimalpain's *VII relacion* we have used a selection (in Chapter 13) describing the demands made by Cortes after the fall of the capital. Finally, there are the *Codex Ramirez,* which includes important data from the informants of Tlatelolco, and the brief sections about the Conquest in the *Anales Tepanecas de Azcapotzalco* and the *Anales de Mexico y Tlatelolco,* both of which are written in Nahuatl.

(6) *Accounts by the native allies of Cortes.* Any presentation of indigenous texts describing the Conquest must contain at least a few of the accounts written by certain historians, Indian and mestizo,[2] descended from those natives who joined with Cortes to defeat the Aztecs. The versions they present of certain events, while differing from the other indigenous narratives, do not fall

outside the general scope of this book. It is true that the Tlaxcaltecas and Tezcocanos fought at the side of the conquistadors, but the effects of the Conquest were as unhappy for them as for the other Nahuas: all were placed under the yoke of Spain, and all lost their ancient culture forever.

Along with the *Lienzo de Tlaxcala* (mentioned previously), we have made use of the *Historia de Tlaxcala* by Diego Munoz Camargo, a mestizo who wrote in Spanish during the second half of the sixteenth century. His obviously slanted version of the massacre at Cholula (in Chapter 5) is particularly interesting. We have also used the descriptions of the Conquest which Don Feranado de Alva Ixtlilxochitl, a descendant of the ruling house of Tezcoco,[3] wrote down from the point of view of the Tezcocanos. His *XIII relacion* and *Historia chichimeca*, both written in Spanish, contain data which he gathered from old Nahuatl sources no longer extant, but which he interpreted in a manner very different from that of the writers of Tenochtitlan and Tlatelolco.

[1] The various Nahuatl-speaking tribes, of whom the Aztecs were by far the most powerful at the time of the Conquest.

[2] Of mixed Indian and Spanish blood.

[3] Three major figures in the history of Tezcoco bore the name "Ixtlilxochitl" and should not be confused. The first was Ixtlilxochitl the Elder (ruled 1409 – 1418), father of the celebrated Nezahualcoyotl (ruled 1418 – 1472); he was killed by Tezozomoc, lord of Azcapotzalco, a city on the western shore of the lake. The second was Hernando Ixtlilxochitl, son of Nezahualpilli (ruled 1472 – 1516) and brother to Cacama (ruled 1516 – 1519), the ruler of Tezcoco at the time of the Conquest. The third, the historian to whom we refer, was a direct descendant.

Postscript:
Reflection on an Unexpected
Historical Account

Histories of confrontations are most often, if not always, written by the winners. And if the defeated are left in precarious circumstances, lacking the means to make their voices heard, it becomes impossible for them to give an account of their history.

In the aftermath of the confrontation between the Amerindians and the Spanish invaders, which the Spaniards described as conquest, most people thought that the vanquished kept silent. Even the well-known Mexican philosopher and politician José Vasconcelos, in a prologue to his *Breve historia de México* (Brief History of Mexico), wrote:

All the happenings of our history are recounted by writers of our language, historians and chroniclers of Spain....And, where is —you may ask—the Indian account? It is easy to answer: how could the poor Indians give an account if they had no means to do so, since they had no written language and did not even know what was happening to them?[1]

Such nonsensical views have not been shared by the majority of historians. This does not mean that they were aware of the accounts of the invasion given in Nahuatl or Maya. Those accounts remained in oblivion for a very long time. Indeed, merely suggesting the possibility of "an Indian account of the conquest" was unexpected, considered naive if not absurd.

The Significance of the Indigenous Accounts

These indigenous texts have to do with an occurrence that radically changed the world-view of the Indians and the Europeans as well. It not only increased, but—for the first time in history—completed the image humankind had of the planet on which they lived. Pointing out the importance for the Europeans of the encounter with the New World, the sixteenth-century Spanish humanist and chronicler Francisco López de Gómara wrote: "After the creation of the world, leaving aside the incarnation and death of the one who created it, the most significant thing has been the discovery of the Indies."[2]

Apart from such theologically colored considerations, the encounter with the unsuspected continent brought about innumerable worldly consequences for the Europeans. Besides the possibility of developing an authentic *imago mundi*, it meant the opportunity to impose political and military hegemony, Christian beliefs, and European language upon millions of people in incredibly vast territories.

It also meant profiting from vast mineral resources—mainly gold and silver—and previously unknown edible, medicinal, and otherwise useful plants. European economic and legal systems, new forms of communication, and agricultural and mineral exploitation developed as never before.

As to the Amerindians, the encounter brought them all sorts of adversities: not only the imposition of a totally different world-view, but the loss of their political, social, religious, and economic structures. The actions perpetrated by the invaders included the destruction of great numbers of monuments, temples, palaces, and images of the gods and ancient rulers. The Aztec metropolis was razed to make way for a new city built along European lines.

Most of the pre-Columbian traditions and other testimonies, including books of paintings and glyphic characters, were lost. In this manner, the Mesoamericans were substantially deprived of their historical memory and even of the possibility of reconstructing it, for their ancient priests and sages had been silenced.

It was in this context that those who had imposed their rule upon the original peoples wrote chronicles, letters, reports, histories, and so on, telling of their deeds. An enormous literature recording the events of the encounter was produced, mainly in Spanish but also in Portuguese, English, French, and even Latin. The literature attracted the attention of thousands who, upon reading it, were motivated to set out for that New World. Among these a good number pursued economic advantage, dreaming of the accumulation of great wealth in a short time. There were also a few motivated by religion: missionaries, mainly Franciscan, Dominican, Augustinian, and Jesuit. From among these one can identify the early chroniclers and some self-taught linguists anxious to learn the natives' languages to facilitate communication with them. Some of these monks did their best to investigate the Amerindian cultures, although mainly with the aim of erasing all traces of what appeared to them idolatry.

Here a question has to be posed again: How could it be that, in these circumstances, some Indians could give testimony on paper, in their own language, of the European invasion and its aftermath?

The Rescue of a Memory

From the European point of view, the encounter meant contact with unexpected and radically different people, but to the Indians, the Europeans' arrival was equally and perhaps even more astonishing. In trying to comprehend the identity of these unknown people, the Amerindians turned to their traditions and myths. Thus, the Aztecs came to believe for a time that Hernán Cortés was Quetzalcóatl, returned with other gods to the land that had originally belonged to them.

The recovery of the Amerindians' memory of the invasion was by no means an easy task. Nor is it easy to discover why or how some Nahua-speaking sages embarked on such an enterprise. We know for sure that among the Nahuas there existed a deep concern for their past. A considerable number of texts, some accompanied by images and glyphic writing, have come down to us. A few were carved in stone, such as the so-called Tizoc Stone, on which the conquests of the Aztec ruler Tizoc are registered by means of images and glyphs. Several other texts appear as alphabetic renditions done some time after the conquest, derived in some cases from pre-Columbian codices or native manuscripts. Suffice it to say that by the third decade of the sixteenth century, a good number of Nahuas and others had learned in the friars' monasteries how to read and write alphabetically. One example of the Nahuas' concern for their past, and of their ability to write about it, is provided by the account of the sixteenth-century chronicler Hernando Alvarado Tezozomoc, a grandson of Motecuhzoma II, who wrote:

Thus they came to pronounce,
thus they set it down in their account,
and they came to draw it on their papers for us,
the old men, the old women.
They were our grandfathers, our grandmothers,
our great-grandfathers, our great-grandmothers,
our great-great-grandfathers, our ancestors,
their account was repeated like a discourse,
they left it for us,
and they bequeathed it
to those of us now living,
to those of us who come from them.

It will never be lost, it will never be forgotten,
that which they came to do,
that which they came to set down in the pictures:
their renown, their history, their memory.
Thus in the future
it will never perish, it will never be forgotten,
we will always keep it,
we their sons, their grandsons,
brothers, great-grandsons, great-great-grandsons,

descendants,
we who have their blood and their color,
we are going to tell it,
we are going to pass it on
to those who are yet to live,
who have yet to be born,
the sons of the Mexicas,
the sons of the Tenochcas.

This ancient oral account,
they left it for us in Mexico,
to be preserved here. . . .

Here, Tenochcas, you will learn
how it started, the renowned, the great city.
Mexico-Tenochtitlan,
in the middle of the waters,
among the reeds, where we live,
where we were born,
we Tenochcas.[3]

The words of Alvarado Tezozomoc's declaration give eloquent testimony to the deep interest the Nahuas had for preserving the memory of their past. And they also provide an example of the mode of preserving it through both the oral tradition and painted books.

Thus the Nahuas rescued from oblivion the memory of the deepest trauma they had experienced in their lives, the one brought by the Spanish invasion: "And all this has happened to us, that which we have seen and beheld. That what has afflicted us and made us so sorrowful and anguished."[4]

The invaders, the cause of their affliction, appeared to their eyes as another type of being, utterly different from them, and the presence of these strangers was not easy to place within their cultural categories. It is true that at first they thought Cortés could be Quetzalcóatl, whose return from the east was expected, and their texts of-

one hundred and eighty-seven

ten use the word *teteo*, "gods," to refer to him and his men. However, the behavior of such "gods" forced the Aztecs to change their minds. When they saw how greedily the Spaniards reacted to gold, the native chroniclers described them as monkeys. And at the end of their writing, they referred to them as *popolocas*, a word whose closest equivalent is "barbarians."

Images of the Other

One salient example is provided by the reports given to Motecuhzoma by the emissaries he had sent to meet Cortés. The Spaniards were introduced to him in these words:

The strangers' bodies are completely covered, so that only their faces can be seen. Their skin is white as if it were made of lime. They have yellow hair, though some of them have black. Their beards are long and yellow and their moustaches are also yellow. Their hair is curly, with very fine strands.

The Spaniards were captured as never before in the images the Nahuas conceived of them. Those images changed for the worse along with the events recorded by the native chroniclers. One recurrent statement was that metal appeared to be attached to both the bodies and souls of the strangers. "Their war gear was made of iron. They dress in iron and wear iron casques. Their swords are iron; their bows are iron; their shields are iron; their spears are iron."[5]

As to what another metal, gold, meant to the strangers, the native account describes how they reacted when the envoy of Motecuhzoma presented many golden objects to them:

They gave the gods ensigns of gold, and ensigns of quetzal feathers and golden necklaces. And when they were given these presents, the Spaniards burst into smiles, their eyes shone with pleasure, they were delighted by them. They picked up the gold and fingered it like monkeys. . . .

The truth is that they longed and lusted for gold. Their bodies swelled with greed, and their hunger was ravenous, they hungered like pigs for that gold.[6]

Similar reactions are described in dealing with the Spaniards' behavior when they were received by Motecuhzoma in a palace in the city of México:

When the Spaniards were installed in the palace, they asked Motecuhzoma about the city's resources and reserves, and about the warriors' ensigns and shields. They questioned him closely and then demanded gold. . . .

When they arrived at the treasure house called Teucalco, the riches of gold and feathers were brought out to them, richly worked shields, disks of gold, necklaces of the gods, gold nose plugs, gold greaves, and bracelets and crowns.

The Spaniards immediately stripped the feathers from the gold shields and ensigns. They gathered all the gold into a great mound and set fire to everything else, regardless of its value. Then they melted down the gold into ingots. The Spaniards grinned like little beasts and patted each other with delight.

When they entered the hall of treasures, it was as if they had arrived in Paradise. They searched everywhere and coveted everything; they were slaves to their own greed.[7]

And not only the Spaniards, but their food and their animals appeared to be perfectly strange. The descriptions offered of the dogs, so different from those small and hairless beasts raised by the Mesoamericans, are revealing.[8] "When Motecuhzoma heard this report, he was filled with terror. It was as if his heart had fainted, as if it had shriveled. It was as if he were conquered by despair."

One last example should be mentioned. It is a description of the courage and ruthlessness of the Spaniards in battle, an attribute comparable—in the eyes of the Aztecs—to their own behavior.

On another occasion the Spaniards entered Atliyacapan. They ransacked the houses and captured a number of prisoners, but when the warriors saw what was happening, they loosed their arrows and rushed forward to attack. The leader of this attack, a valiant chief named Axoquentzin, pressed the enemy so hard that they were forced to release their prisoners and drop all their spoils. But this great chief died when a Spanish sword entered his breast and found his heart.[8]

Epic narrative of battles, stupor at seeing the behavior of others never before imagined—all this and much more that captivates the attention is the substance out of which the vision of the vanquished is composed. Recall how the narrative begins with the wonders, signs, and omens foretelling the arrival of the Spaniards.

The Beginning and End of the Aztec Account

People were amazed and frightened, so the text asserts, when they saw a fiery signal that appeared in the sky. It seemed that the Main Temple burst into flames, and another temple was struck by a bolt of lightning. Fire streamed through the sky while the sun still shone. The wind lashed the lake's water until it boiled. The Mother Goddess was heard weeping at night. Motecuhzoma was also affected by the omens. A bird was captured in the lake, and a strange mirror was found on its head. Motecuhzoma looked in the mirror and saw people coming forward on the backs of animals resembling deer. Increasing the people's fright, monstrous beings were seen in the city, deformed men with two heads. Wonders indeed! The strange happenings, imagined or true, recalled by the Nahua chroniclers became a sort of ominous prologue to the story.

And at the very end of it, the epic account recalls other omens. Enormous spirals, like a whirlwind, gave off a shower of sparks and red-hot coals. They anticipated the Aztec surrender after eighty days of siege in the city. So the vision of the vanquished was conceived and put down in alphabetical writing.

The Story Continues

It seemed that with the Aztec nation crushed, driven to the ground, all had been lost. But the ultimate truth is different. Those who survived the affliction of plagues and forced labor, although greatly reduced in numbers, managed to preserve the core of their culture, their language, their true being.

The last chapter of this book, Aftermath, offers evidence of the fate of the vanquished. Employing several texts, some of them never published before, it gives glimpses of what happened to them during almost five centuries that followed the Aztec surrender. The unexpected historical account thus arrives at the present. Although contemporary life is merely touched upon with this chapter, it provides enough light to enable the reader to ponder the drama and the tragedy. Two poems included at the very end appear to have been conceived as an invitation to the natives to proceed beyond the darkness.

Could the descendants of the vanquished learn to trust in themselves? The unexpected has arrived. Now we know that the ancient wisdom is blossoming again. Voices of hope are heard, not voices asking for mercy, but demanding voices. The descendants of those who first settled in the Americas will no more be vanquished. The time has come for them to live side by side with the other members of society, preserving and enriching, as they wish, all that can be meaningful to them on the earth.

[1] José Vasconcelos, *Breve Historia de México* (México: Editorial Botas, 1936), p. 10.

[2] Francisco López de Gómara, *Historia general de las Indias* (Zaragoza: Casa de Miguel Millán, 1552), folio II v.

[3] Hernando Alvarado Tezozomoc, *Crónica Mexicayotl* (México: National University Press, 1975), pp. 4–6.

[4] "Annales of Tlatelolco," Mexican Manuscript 22, National Library of France, folio 34.

[5] See chapter 3, p. 30.

[6] See chapter 6, p. 51.

[7] See chapter 8, pp. 66 and 68.

[8] See chapter 12, p. 110.

Selected Bibliography

1. Primary Sources

Anales de Mexico y Tlatelolco. (Indian Annals of Tlatelolco and Mexico, from 1473 to 1521.) Preserved at the National Museum of Anthropology, Mexico City.

Anonymous Manuscript of Tlatelolco (1528). Preserved at the National Library of Paris. Facsimile edition published by Ernst Mengin in *Corpus Codicum Americanorum Medii Aevi*, vol. II, Copenhagen, 1945.

Atlas o Codice de Duran in *Historia de las Indias de la Nueva Espana e Islas de Tierra Firme*, by Fray Diego de Duran, Porrúa, Mexico, 1968.

Cantares Mexicanos (Collection of Mexican Indian Songs). Sixteenth-century manuscript preserved at the National Library of Mexico. Facsimile reproduction published by Antonio Peñafiel, Oficina Tipografica de Secretaria de Fomento, Mexico, 1904. See also *Poesía Nahuatl*, vols. 2 and 3, with an introduction, paleography, and translation into Spanish by Angel M. Garibay K. Universidad Nacional, Mexico, 1965–1967. Numerous compositions taken from this manuscript, translated into English, are included in Miguel Leon-Portilla, *Pre-Columbian Literatures of Mexico*, Norman: University of Oklahoma Press, 1968.

Chimalpain Quauhtlehuanitzin, Francisco de San Anton Munon, *Sixième et Septième Relations* (1258–1612). Publiées et traduites sur le manuscrit original par Remi Simeon. Maisoneuve et Ch. Leclerc, Paris, 1889.

Codice Aubin (or Codex 1576). Ed. and trans. by Ch. E. Dibble. Chimalytac, Madrid, 1963.

Codice Florentino. 3 vols. Facsimile edition published by the Mexican government, Mexico, 1979.

Codice Ramirez, "Relacion del origen de los indios que habitan esta Nueva Espana segun sus historias" (A fragment on *Noticias relativas a la conquista desde la llegada de Cortes a Tetzcuco hasta la toma del Templo Mayor de Mexico*, bound together with the "Ramirez Codex.") Editorial Leyenda, Mexico, 1944.

Florentine Codex. General History of the Things of New Spain, Fray Bernardino de Sahagun. Books I–XII, trans. from Nahuatl into English by Arthur J. O. Anderson and Charles E. Dibble. 12 vols. School of American Research and the University of Utah, Santa Fe, New Mexico, 1950–1982.

Informantes indigenas de Sahagun, *Historia de la Conquista.* (See Florentine Codex.)

Ixtlilxochitl, Fernando de Alva, *Obras Historicas.* 2 vols. National University, Mexico, 1975–1977.

Lienzo de Tlaxcala. Antiguedades mexicanas, published by Junta Colombina de Mexico en el IV Centenario del Descubrimiento de America. 2 vols. Oficina de la Secretaria de Fomento, Mexico, 1892. Also: Papel y Cartón, Mexico, 1983.

Muñoz Camargo, Diego, *Historia de Tlaxcala.* Ed. Chavero, Mexico, 1892.

Tezozomoc, F. Alvarado, *Cronica mexicana.* Ed. de Vigil, printed by Editorial Leyenda, Mexico, 1944.

——, *Cronica mexicayotl.* Paleography and translation into Spanish by Adrian Leon. Imprenta Universitaria, Mexico, 1975.

II. Other References

Acosta, Joseph de, *Historia natural y moral de las indias.* Fondo de Cultura Economica, Mexico, 1986.

Aguilar, Fray Francisco de, *Historia de la Nueva Espana.* 2d. ed. rev. by Alfonso Teja Zabre. Ediciones Botas, Mexico, 1938.

Amaya Topete, Jesus, *Atlas mexicano de la conquista.* Fondo de Cultura Economica, Mexico, 1958.

Anonymous Conqueror. *Narrative of Some Things of New Spain and the Great City of Temestitan, Mexico.* Trans. into English by Marshall H. Saville (*Documents and Narratives Concerning the Discovery and Conquest of Latin America*, no. 1, Cortes Society, New York, 1917).

Bancroft, Hubert Howe, *The Conquest of Mexico.* New York, 1883.

Boban, Eugene, *Documents pour servir à l'Histoire du Mexique.* Catalogue Raisonné de la Collection de M. E. Eugène Goupil, Paris, 1891.

Braden, C. S., *Religious Aspects of the Conquest of Mexico.* Duke University Press, Durham, 1930.

Casas, Fray Bartolome de las, *Brevisima relacion de la destruccion de las Indias.* Madrid, 1879.

Caso, Alfonso, *The People of the Sun.* University of Oklahoma Press, Norman, 1986.

Codex Borbonicus. A pre-Columbian Codex preserved in the Library of the Chamber of Deputies. Commentary by Karl A. Novotny. Akademische Druck- und Verlag Anstalt, Graz, 1974.

Codex Borgia. A pre-Columbian Codex preserved in the Ethnographical Museum of the Vatican, Rome. 3 vols. Fondo de Cultura, Mexico, 1982.

Codex Mendoza (Mendocino). Ed. and trans. by James Cooper Clark. London, 1938.

Motolinia, Fray Toribio, *History of the Indians of New Spain*. Trans. and ed. by Elizabeth Andros Foster. Cortes Society, Berkeley, 1950. (Documents and Narrative Concerning the Discovery and Conquest of Latin America, new series, no. 4.)

Orozco y Berra, Manuel, *Historia antigua y de la conquista de Mexico*. With a previous study by Angel M. Garibay K., the author's biography, and three bibliographies by Miguel Leon-Portilla. 4 vols. Porrúa, Mexico, 1960.

Prescott, William, *History of the Conquest of Mexico*. Ed. by John Foster Kirks. Ruskin House, Allen and Unwin Ltd., London, 1949.

Radin, Paul, *The Sources and Authenticity of the History of the Ancient Mexicans*. University of California Press, Berkeley, 1920. (University of California Publications in American Archaeology and Ethnology, vol. 17, no. 1.)

Robertson, Donald, *Mexican Manuscript Painting of the Early Colonial Period*. Yale University Press, New Haven, 1959.

Sahagun, Fray Bernardino de, *Codex Florentino:* Illustrations for Sahagun's *Historia General de las Cosas de Nueva Espana*. Ed. by Francisco del Paso y Troncoso, vol. V. Madrid, 1905.

——, *General History of the Things of New Spain* (Florentine Codex), Books I–IX and XII, trans. from Aztec into English by Arthur J. O. Anderson and Charles E. Dibble. School of American Research and the University of Utah, Santa Fe, New Mexico, 1950–1982.

——, *Historia general de las cosas de Nueva Espana*. Books I–IV trans. by Fanny Bandelier. Nashville, 1932.

Seler, Eduard, *Gesammelte Abhandlungen zur Amerikanischen Sprach und Altertumskunde*. 5 vols. Ascher und Co. (and) Behrend und Co., Berlin, 1902–1923. Facsimile reproduction, Akademische Druck- und Verlag Anstalt, Graz.

Tapia, Andres de, "Relacion sobre la conquista de Mexico," in *Coleccion de Documentos para la Historia de Mexico*, published by J. G. Icazbalceta. T. II. Mexico, 1866.

Vaillant, George C., *The Aztecs of Mexico. Origin, Rise and Fall of the Aztec Nation*. Penguin Books, London, 1986.

Vázquez de Tapia, Bernardino, *Relacion del conquistador*. Published by Manuel Romero de Terreros, Editorial Polis, Mexico, 1944.

Yáñez, Agustin, *Cronicas de la conquista*. Biblioteca del Estudiante Universitario. No. 2. 8th ed. National University of Mexico Press, Mexico, 1982.

Coleccion de documentos para la historia de Mexico. Compiled by Joaquin Garcia Icazbalceta. Mexico, 1858–1866.

Conway, G. R. G., *La Noche Triste*, Documentos: Segura de la Frontera en Nueva Espana, año de 1520. Gante Press, Mexico, 1943.

Cortes, Hernan, *Letters of Cortes*. Trans. and ed. by F. A. MacNutt. New York and London, 1908.

Diaz del Castillo, Bernal, *The Discovery and Conquest of Mexico*. Trans. with an introduction and notes by A. P. Maudslay (1908). Farrar, Straus, and Cudahy, New York, 1956.

Duran, Fray Diego, *Historia de las Indias de Nueva Espana e Islas de Tierra Firme*. 2 vols. and atlas. Introduction by A. M. Garibay. Porrúa, Mexico, 1968.

Fernandez de Oviedo, Gonzalo, *Historia general y natural de las Indias, Islas y Tierra Firme*. 4 vols. Madrid, 1851–1855.

Garibay K., Angel M., *Historia de la Literatura Nahuatl* (A History of Nahuatl Literature). 2 vols. Porrúa, Mexico, 1953–1954. A fundamental work on the literary creations of the various Nahuatl-speaking groups of ancient Mexico.

——, *Veinte Himnos Sacros de las Nahuas* (Twenty Sacred Hymns of the Nahuas). Fuentes Indigenas de la Cultura Nahuatl. Informantes Indigenas de Sahagun, 2. Introduction, paleography, translation, and commentary by Seminario de Cultura Nahuatl. Instituto de Historia, National University of Mexico Press, 1958.

Gibson, Charles, *Tlaxcala in the Sixteenth Century*. Yale University Press, New Haven, 1952.

Gomara, Francisco Lopez de, *Historia de la Conquista de Mexico*. Introduction and notes by Joaquin Ramirez Cabañas. 2 vols. Editorial Robredo, Mexico, 1945.

Kingsborough, Lord, *Antiquities of Mexico*. 9 vols. London, 1831–1848.

Lehmann, Walter, "Die Geschichte der Königreiche von Colhuacan und Mexico" (The Annals of Cuauhtitlan), *Quellenwerke zur alten Geschichte Amerikas*, Bd. I. Text mit Ubersetzung von Walter Lehmann. Stuttgart, 1938.

Leon-Portilla, Miguel, *Aztec Thought and Culture: A Study of the Ancient Nahuatl Mind*. University of Oklahoma Press, Norman, 1963.

——, *Pre-Columbian Literatures of Mexico*. University of Oklahoma Press, Norman, 1968.

——, *Native Mesoamerican Spirituality*. Paulist Press, New York, 1988.

Martir de Angleria, Pedro, *Decadas del Nuevo Mundo*. Editorial Bajel, Buenos Aires, 1944.

Mendieta, Fray Jeronimo de, *Historia eclesiastica indiana*. 4 vols. Editorial Salvador Chavez Hayhoe, Mexico, 1945.

Index

two hundred and one